Defending the Wilderness

A York State
BOOKS

Adirondack Virgin Forest.

Defending the WILDERNESS

THE ADIRONDACK WRITINGS
OF PAUL SCHAEFER

Paul Schaefer

SYRACUSE UNIVERSITY PRESS

First Edition, 1989
94 93 92 91 90 89   6 5 4 3 2 1

This book is published with the assistance
of a grant from the John Ben Snow Foundation.

The paper used in this publication meets the minimum requirements of
American National Standard for Information Sciences—Permanence of
Paper for Printed Library Materials, ANSI Z39.48-1984. ∞™

Library of Congress Cataloging-in-Publication Data

Schaefer, Paul.
  Defending the wilderness.

  (A York State book)
  1. Nature conservation—New York (State)—Adirondack
Park.   2. Nature conservation—New York (State)—
Adirondack Forest Preserve.   3. Nature conservation—
New York (State)—Adirondack Mountain Reserve.
4. Adirondack Park (N.Y.)   5. Adirondack Forest
Preserve (N.Y.)   6. Adirondack Mountain Reserve (N.Y.)
7. Schaefer, Paul. I. Title.
QH76.5.N7S33   1989   338.78'2'0974753   89-4376
ISBN 0-8156-0236-7 (alk. paper)
ISBN 0-8156-0237-5 (pbk. : alk. paper)

MANUFACTURED IN THE UNITED STATES OF AMERICA

Dedicated to the Memories of

JOHN S. APPERSON

whose vision, courage, and indefatigable actions on behalf of the New York State Forest Preserve in the Adirondack and Catskill mountains inspired all who knew him,

and to

HOWARD ZAHNISER

inimitable friend and wilderness companion, who incorporated the essence of the "forever wild" covenant of the New York State Forest Preserve into the National Wilderness Preservation Act of 1964, of which he was the author.

PAUL SCHAEFER has been a visionary leader of the New York State conservation movement since his early twenties. During his long career, he has served on countless advisory committees for state and private agencies. His numerous awards and honors include the Chevron USA Conservation Award (1986), the Governor Mario Cuomo Conservation Award (1985), the Conservationist of the Year Award from the Adirondack Council (1985), the Conservationist of the Year Award from International Safari (1969), and the Governor's Award from the New York State Conservation Council (1966). He was involved with the passage of the National Wilderness Act of 1964 and for eleven years was the editor of the *Forest Preserve*. In 1979, Union College recognized his outstanding contributions to conservation by awarding him an honorary doctor of science degree.

Contents

Illustrations

Foreword

CHARLES CALLISON

Right now, as this volume is published, the remaining unspoiled wilderness of the Adirondacks—the true, roadless wilderness areas, a million-plus acres, as officially designated —seems secure for all time. Thus its most indefatigable advocate and defender for most of this century is content to wrap the core of his records and testimony between the covers of a book.

How and why secure? The history is here. First there was, and remains, the "forever wild" guarantee of the New York State Forest Preserve written into the Constitution of New York in 1894, a guarantee held fast by the people of the state through a series of political struggles, some prolonged and bitter. Then there are landmark court decisions, standing like the great rocks of the mountains, and from time to time legislative acts and executive rulings that clarified the definitions and tightened the protection. Finally, the Adirondack Park Agency Act of 1971 and subsequent ratification by the legislature of wilderness and wild and scenic river designations; and also a master plan for the private lands within the "blue line" boundary of the six-million-acre park, a worthy model for the nation. These latter were the culmination of a series of legislative committee and commission studies in which Paul Schaefer played central and strategic roles.

There is another reason for his and our confidence. It is the continuing watchfulness of organizations like the venerable but still vital Association for the Protection of the Adirondacks (APA) and the younger Adirondack Council, a coalition of strong groups.

Introduced to the Adirondacks at the age of 12 and growing rapidly into a tall and sinewy man, Paul quickly acquired the skills of woodsman and hunter. While still in his teens the former city lad had been accepted into the fraternity of native guides. Then he discovered Verplank Colvin's 1873 report to the legislature on his pioneering survey and straightway became a disciple of Colvin, determined himself to explore the "mystery" of the mountains that Colvin sensed, the "oneness" of the region that Colvin perceived long before the scientific understanding of ecosystems, and dedicated to preservation of the great preserve and park that Colvin had called for as early as 1872.

When only twenty-three Paul was drawn into a circle of activists led by John S. Apperson, who instructed him in the ways to organize for a cause and how to reach out to public opinion. As the decades passed, others may have been up front in the halls of legislation or courts of law, but it was Paul Schaefer who was their coach, their cheerleader, their pamphleteer, and their supplier of facts, facts gleaned not only from books but firsthand on innumerable hikes and camping trips into remote reaches of the great region, as often carrying a camera as a fishing rod or a deer rifle. Sometimes, as necessary, he was very up front himself, as when he served as president of the Adirondack Hudson River Association and assembled a massive coalition to crush "Gooley No. 1 Dam" and shut the dam builders out of the Hudson basin within the "blue line."

Sometimes by the very force of his determination he kept wavering allies in the battle. When confronted by a decision of the New York State Conservation Commissioner to permit a major dam on the Moose River, a ruling said to be beyond appeal, he went with colleague Ed Richard to New York City to seek the help of the powerful APA. The Association's legal minds couldn't figure out what to do—"no way to appeal." In cold fury the two walked out, Schaefer delivering the parting shot: "Well, we are going to fight!" These events are not recorded here, but are told by Frank Graham in his *Adirondack Park: A Political History* (1978).

Schaefer and Richard found a way to appeal—over the heads of commissioner and courts—to the people of New York. The APA joined in.

He writes of his encounters with national conservation leaders, among them the legendary Bob Marshall, founder of the Wilderness Society, and Marshall's successor, the scholarly and eloquent Howard Zahniser, author of the National Wilderness Preservation Act. He was inspired by them and they in turn, I know, were heartened by Paul's own enthusiasm and intensity.

Paul Schaefer, now in his own ninth decade, is convinced that the Adirondack Mountains will never be completely explored or understood, at least not by any one person, no matter how ardent and indefatigable, in a long lifetime. "Even in this thought," he muses, "there is a certain richness." Paul Schaefer has probably come as close to seeing all of it than anyone ever did, and worked harder to save it—all the while making a living as a craftsman and builder of quality early American homes.

The grandeur and enduring mystery of New York's "great northern wilderness" have inspired a mountain of literature. Some of that mountain is pap, much of it scientific and documentary, some of it genuinely good writing. It is fitting that Paul Schaefer has added significantly to it. Here is history, but more than history, here is the personal testimony of a man's love for a wild land and his unflagging determination to preserve it.

Preface

Around 1930 an unprecedented series of attacks were made upon the integrity of the New York State Forest Preserve in the Adirondack and Catskill mountains. The issue was either to maintain the wild-forest character of these mountains or to modify/eliminate the ironclad protection that these state lands enjoyed since 1894 under the now-famous "forever wild" covenant of the New York State Constitution.

The essays in this book were written over a period of fifty years and were published on an average of about one every year and a half. Each article was meant for specific audiences in light of the constantly changing legal, legislative, and public happenings. As a builder of traditional homes, I was usually under great business pressure, since I usually had a half-dozen jobs under way simultaneously and twenty or more craftsmen working for me. But the Adirondacks always came first. When a problem surfaced, I would leave the jobs in the best hands possible and come home and pound the typewriter until the point I had in mind had been expressed and the resulting article had been sent to the press, magazines, wire service, or to my own publication the *Forest Preserve*.

During those years, I found that words crystallized and took on a luster far beyond their dictionary meanings when illustrated with photographs. No combination of words could describe the beauty of virgin forest in Moose River country or the devastation of Wolf Mountain by forest fire. Yet if you compare photographs of each (both are in the text) side by side, the images formed in the mind present us with a choice of either protecting nature or allowing it to be destroyed. The emotions that the combination of words and pictures evoke are so powerful they impel us into action.

From early on I carried a camera wherever I went and recorded on film, first in black and white and more recently in color, places and people of the Adirondacks. Most of the photographs in this book were taken in the Adirondack wild country during our efforts to define wilderness, and they were used to strengthen the image of our wonderful natural heritage that would be lost if the "forever wild" covenant was weakened. In addition to my own photographs, I have included many that were taken by individuals (credited throughout the book) who have permitted me over the years to use their work to supplement my own extensive collection.

Another dimension of photography that became very important in our campaign to preserve Adirondack wild country was the motion picture. No one I ever met advocated its use more than conservationist John S. Apperson. Within weeks after my first meeting with him in 1931, he put Dr. Irving Langmuir's 16-mm Bell and Howell camera in my hands. "Take this," he said, "Go up to Tahawus and shoot the lumbering operation and the marvelous country it ruined. We will wake them all up." When we reached Tahawas several days later, a major crown forest fire was sweeping across the highway, across Lake Sanford, across the Opalescent River to to the top of North River Mountain.

The silent, black-and-white documentary film we helped to produce for Apperson in 1931 and 1932 does not compare to the sound-and-color films of today. But then, no one else was using film to help win conservation battles, and the medium was amazingly successful. A few years later, in 1945, again we used a motion picture, some of it shot in color, to help win the eleven-year battle over the South Branch of the Moose River.

While my days behind a motion-picture camera were limited, I recognized the value that film had in educating people about the forest preserve and have used it to advantage through the years. In 1970, *Of Rivers and Men* played an important part in the effort to get the Wild, Scenic, and Recreational Rivers System Act a part of New York state policy.

The success of *Of Rivers and Men* spawned another film *The Adirondack—The Land Nobody Knows*, which was completed in 1980. The full effect of this film is not yet known. Its worldwide exposure and its presentation to thousands of audiences, notably in schools, has had as great an impact on the Adirondack Forest Preserve as any other single contribution that I can think of during the last half century. The latter film was made through the efforts of countless volunteers who donated their time and skills for years—especially photographers Walt Haas and Ed Niedhammer and writer/editor Noel Riedinger-Johnson.

Looking back on these last fifty years—when it often seemed the country we loved so much was about to be destroyed—I have to say honestly that they were some of the finest times of my life. The frequent trips into the wilderness and the innumerable—and often exhausting—barnstorming trips across the state gave a powerful meaning to the ideas I tried to express in the articles I wrote, which appear here with only some minor adjustments and updatings. Somehow during those years the houses got built, the jobs finished, the men paid. And somehow it seemed that our efforts to keep the "forever wild" covenant intact developed into a philosophy that became consistently stronger.

I would not have been able to devote the time and effort over the years without the support of my family, who understood my devotion to the Adirondack lowlands and saw the splendor of forests, rivers, and lakes from the summits of all the high peaks and many lesser ones; the many individuals who unselfishly devoted their lives to the New York State Forest Preserve; the New York State Conservation Council with its hundreds of thousands of sportsmen across the state; the many organizations and associations that came together in political support of "forever wild"; and the statesmen who made possible our fondest aspirations. I appreciate the editorial assistance of Noel Riedinger-Johnson who helped compile this collection of articles that document our campaign of more than a half century to preserve wilderness in the Adirondacks.

Teddy Roosevelt once said it all in just a few words: "Aggressive fighting for the right is the noblest sport the world affords."

Schenectady, New York
Fall 1988

PAUL SCHAEFER

The lands of the state, now owned or hereafter acquired, constituting the forest preserve as now fixed by law, shall be forever kept as wild forest lands. They shall not be leased, sold or exchanged, or be taken by any corporation, public or private, nor shall the timber thereon be sold, removed or destroyed.

Article XIV Section I
New York State Constitution

Association for the Protection of the Adirondacks

Article XIV, Section 1.

The Covenant

Protection of New York State's watershed mountains was given in 1885 under a statute law when the New York State Legislature created the New York State Forest Preserve and appointed the forest commission to administer state lands in the Adirondack Mountains. In 1892 the legislature approved the forest commission's proposal to designate 2,807,000 acres of land in the Adirondacks, delineated by a blue pencil line on a state map and commonly referred to as the "blue line," to become the Adirondack Park. This contained both the state lands of the preserve as well as those privately held. When the forest commission failed in its duties to oversee the state lands by selling or leasing prime wild lands to lumber interests, the public, as represented by members of the 1894 New York State Constitutional Convention, took away the commission's powers and invested control of these lands to the people of the state in the now-famous "forever wild" constitutional covenant.

This constitutional provision can be changed only by the affirmative action of two successive legislatures followed by a referendum of the people in election time. Although it has been under almost constant attack by commercial interests since 1895 when it went into effect, this covenant has been sustained for nearly one hundred years by the people in constitutional conventions and by the New York State Court of Appeals in many diverse decisions.

This unique covenant protects critically important watershed forests at the sources of the state's principal rivers and streams. It prevents unnecessary highway and reservoir construction that would devastate prime river and lake basins and the wildlife thereon. And it bans all manners of usages contrary to the preservation of natural wild-forest conditions.

Today the Adirondack Park contains nearly six million acres of land and is the largest park in the contiguous United States. It is larger than the state of Massachusetts, larger than the combined areas of Yellowstone, Yosemite, Grand Canyon, Glacier, and Olympic national parks. The Adirondack Forest Preserve has grown to more than 2.6 million acres within the "blue line" boundary of the park, which is protected by Article XIV, Section 1, of the state constitution.

More than a million acres in the forest preserve are designated as wilderness and primitive regions. The remaining one and a half million acres are specified as wild-forest areas and differ only in that they lack the ban against motor vehicles and planes, which the wilderness and primitive regions enjoy. There is enough land to identify additional areas that exhibit unique ecological diversity, including another major natural area in the northwest portion of the park. A system of wild, scenic, and recreational rivers assures the free-flowing character of more than twelve hundred miles of the state's finest rivers.

In the forest preserve, scores of public campsites, awe-inspiring mountains, magnificent lakes and streams, and challenging white-water rivers afford limitless opportunities for camping, hiking, backpacking, canoeing, rafting, swimming, hunting, fishing, skiing, snowshoeing, and many other outdoor activities. None of these activities interfere with the primary goal of the New York State Forest Preserve, which is the protection of the vital sources of our principal rivers and streams—the great watershed forests on the mountains and in the fragile wild areas.

Many of the individuals who have fought to retain the integrity of the forest preserve generally agree that the best use of land in the Adirondack Park will be when slightly more than three million acres are constitutionally protected forest preserve lands and slightly less acreage is in private ownership and commercial entities. It is hoped that the open spaces of the private lands will complement the wild-forest character of the state land. Protection of the back country will be encouraged through the use of conservation easements.

With all its outstanding attributes, the park is still large enough to accommodate great open-space estates and hundreds of thousands of acres of forest lands commercially harvested by lumber and paper companies. There is room enough for university campuses totaling tens of thousands of acres to conduct forestry and wildlife studies and for the Olympic Authority to run two major ski centers, one with the highest vertical drop in the East, not to mention other private ski centers. Many villages and hamlets dot the park with a resident population of more than 100,000 people. Many of these inhabitants belong to families who have lived in the Adirondacks for generations, and they embody the fortitude of this vital region.

But for all its present uses and protections, the park needs a watchful eye over future planning—especially regarding land use for people and for commercial establishment serving the tourist industry. Most important the people of the state must continue their sentinel of the New York State Forest Preserve and Article XIV, Section 1, of the New York State Constitution. For a hundred years, there have been philosophical disagreements over this treasured land. These will continue. Ultimately the more persuasive arguments will crystallize, and the Adirondacks will continue to be one of the most unique places on planet Earth.

Defending the Wilderness

1

Adirondack Wilderness

O.K. Slip Falls. "We cannot set aside wilderness for a decade or two, merely until we want to use it for other purposes. The essence of wilderness preservation is perpetuity." —William M. Foss, Assistant Commissioner for Lands and Forests, New York State Conservation Department, 1959.

As the year 1984 was drawing to a close and the New York State Forest Preserve Centennial Celebration was approaching in 1985, numerous excellent short histories about the Adirondacks and the Catskills were being published. None of them contained a chronological record of the way wilderness regions evolved within the New York State Forest Preserve.

Since wildness is the essence of what the forest preserve represents, it seemed important to recount the movement that transformed much of the wild forest lands protected by the New York State Constitution into genuine wilderness regions. I was asked to write an article for the centennial issue of the *New York State Conservationist*. "The Making of a Wilderness," appeared in the May 1985 issue of the magazine. This essay is essentially in the form originally submitted for publication and includes material that was edited out because of duplication of facts appearing in other articles in that issue.

Looking back a hundred years, the New York State Forest Preserve was established when state lands in the Adirondack and Catskill mountains were set aside and given "forever wild" protection through statute law in 1885. Devastating lumbering operations in these regions and the resulting forest fires had destroyed critical watershed forests and seriously diminished the flow of water in rivers and streams. A serious drought in 1883 had compounded the problem. Continued mismanagement of these lands by appointed officials between 1885 and 1894 caused the original "forever wild" statute to be placed within the new New York State Constitution, which went into effect in 1895. This action took control of the forest preserve from state officials and vested it in the hands of the people, where it has remained.

The debates that led to the "forever wild" constitutional covenant emphasized the preservation of watershed forests at the sources of our principal rivers and streams. Among these rivers were the Hudson, Mohawk, Black, Oswegatchie, Beaver, Raquette, Saranac, and Ausable. The philosophy of watershed forest protection dominated the efforts of preservationists in their innumerable battles to protect the covenant for more than three decades.

This new protection, even without specific guidelines, seemed to be doing an adequate job of protecting the forest preserve until 1932 when state officials approved construction of a bobsled run on state lands for the Olympics. The proposal was challenged by the Association for the Protection of the Adirondacks on principles espoused by Louis Marshall, the brilliant constitutional lawyer and delegate to the New York State Constitutional Conventions of both 1894 and 1915, who helped to write the "forever wild" article. In upholding the association's position, the Court of Appeals unanimously held that: "We must preserve it [the forest preserve] in its wild state, its trees, its rocks, its streams. . . . It must always retain the character of a wilderness."

At that time aircraft and motor vehicles were beginning to penetrate some of the most remote regions of the forest preserve, and there were no clear-cut regulations prohibiting such use. Wilderness potential in the Adirondacks was being eroded despite the constitutional covenant, which was ambiguous in this regard. In 1932 a proposal for the construction of closed cabins with access roads and appurtenances, having been approved by two successive legislatures as required by law, came before the people for decision. If approved, wilderness was doomed. But last minute all-out efforts by conservationists, supported by key public officials and statesmen, killed it. Out of that close call and resounding victory came the conservation movement that sought to really protect and enhance the wilderness in both the Adirondack and Catskill parks.

The February 1930 issue of *Scientific Monthly* carried an article entitled "The Problem of the Wilderness." This four-thousand-word article was written by Robert Marshall, Louis Marshall's son, who had spent his youth with his brother and a guide climbing Adirondack mountains and who had obtained his initial forestry education on the Adirondack campus of the Syracuse College of Forestry. Marshall espoused the cause of wilderness in a manner that had never been done before. A wilderness philosophy as such was not really new. Henry David Thoreau, John Muir, Aldo Leopold, and others voiced in their best language wilderness values. But Marshall used the words that fitted the era in which he lived: a time when the mechanization and pollution of the nation was becoming more and more visible, a time when it appeared that unless the heedless rush of civilization could be curbed the priceless entity of wilderness would be lost forever. He ended that article with words that have sounded the tocsin ever since:

> It is exigent that all friends of the wilderness ideal unite. If they do
> not present the urgency of their viewpoint the other side will cer-

tainly capture popular support. Then it will be only a few years until the last escape from society will be barricaded. If that day arrives there will be countless souls born to live in strangulation, countless human beings who will be crushed under the artificial edifice raised by man. There is just one hope of repulsing the tyrannical ambition of civilization to conquer every niche on the whole earth. That hope is the organization of spirited people who will fight for the freedom of the wilderness.

I had met Marshall on the top of Mount Marcy in July, 1932. At that chance meeting, Marshall learned of the pending closed cabin amendment and saw firsthand the extensive lumbering of virgin forest on Mount Adams. Visibly upset, Marshall restated the need for like-minded people who loved the wilderness to band together and fight for wilderness preservation.

In 1935 Marshall organized the Wilderness Society with the help of seven other people. Two years later he wrote another classic article entitled "The Vanishing Wilderness" with the awesome, deathless words bringing urgent, new life to those who had experienced wilderness.

A young man employed by the federal government in Washington was one of those who clearly heard the call that Marshall had sounded. His name was Howard Zahniser. He left a more lucrative job to become the executive secretary of the Wilderness Society. He and I first met at the showing of a film on the Moose River in 1946, deep in the canyons of New York City. When he learned that the Moose River Plains and the largest deer wintering yard was about to be flooded, he pledged support to help stop construction of the planned dam. He agreed to come to the Adirondacks at an early date; he had never been there before. In August of that year he and I, along with Ed Richard who was heading the Moose River fight, made a seventeen-mile hike that ended at my ancient log cabin on the edge of what is now the Siamese Ponds Wilderness. He asked me to find a cabin for him and his family, and I located one about a quarter of a mile from mine at two-thousand-feet elevation, from which he could look across miles of what was to become a land he loved above all others. His nearest neighbor to the west was thirteen miles distant, across a wild land of mountains, forests, lakes, and streams. It meant, also, that we would be able to meet frequently. He became deeply involved in our many battles over the Adirondacks.

The state legislature had created the Joint Legislative Committee on Natural Resources for New York State in 1950. Composed of distinguished members of both the senate and assembly, it also had sixteen advisory members representing a broad spectrum of business as well as conservation interests. Along with men representing lumber and power interests were such men as Karl T. Frederick, founder of the New York State Conservation Council; Lithgow Osborne, respected commissioner of the New York State Conservation Department for ten years; and Gustave Swanson, head of the Cornell University Department of Natural Sciences. I served on the committee for fifteen years.

On January 2, 1953, Howard Zahniser was requested to present his views of the Adirondacks in national perspective before this legislative committee in Albany. It was a memorable and inspiring speech that brought out the richness of wilderness possibilities in the Adirondacks. A month later he introduced in the United States Congress the first draft of the National Wilderness Preservation Act, which he authored. His presentation to the committee included the following statement: "My work as executive secretary of the Wilderness Society . . . has taken me far and away to great and beautiful wilderness areas throughout the country, and I can testify with assurance that here, within practical reach of some twenty millions of people are some of the loveliest wilderness retreats left in the United States."

Six more years passed with the New York State Joint Legislative Committee on Natural Resources meeting monthly and with members of the committee taking extended trips into the Adirondacks before the question of wilderness was to become a serious item on the agenda. At the December 2, 1959, meeting in Albany, Chairman Robert Watson Pomeroy stated that when he assumed chairmanship of the committee, he had initiated the study of wilderness in the Adirondacks and said that he would soon begin a similar study in the Catskills. He reported that at a meeting held at Shattuc Clearing in the High Peak country on September 9–11, 1959, Neil Stout, executive director of the committee, and Clarence Petty, a forester assigned to Stout from the Conservation Department by Commissioner Harold Wilm, recommended wilderness designation of eight areas with plans to add more. During the meeting in Albany on that December 2d, J. Victor Skiff, deputy commissioner of the Conservation Department said: "I have reported previously that at a special meeting held early in the spring with Chairman Pomeroy, Commissioner Wilm, and myself, a decision resulted in regard to Adirondack and Catskill Forest Preserve areas. We have decided to leave the wilderness part of the survey pretty much up to this committee."

William M. Foss, assistant commissioner for Lands and Forests of the Conservation Department and a dedicated consultant for the New

York State Joint Legislative Committee on Natural Resources, followed that statement by saying: "I think everyone here will agree to the desirability of preserving for future generations the true wilderness areas. I would like to point out that we cannot set aside wilderness for a decade or two, merely until we want to use it for other purposes. The essence of wilderness preservation is perpetuity; zoning for wilderness must keep this in mind."

Dean Hardy Shirley of the Syracuse College of Forestry concluded: "I want to say first that I am personally delighted with the type of report we had this morning on the designation of wilderness areas, and I think it is an absolutely essential step if we are not to lose the entire character of the Adirondack Forest Preserve and the whole Adirondack Park."

The work of the committee received vital support from Lieutenant Governor Frank C. Moore and Assembly Speaker Oswald D. Heck and reflected the political strength conservationists had secured through a series of legislative actions and constitutional amendments. Supplementing this was the growing support for wilderness at the national level and in Congress, resulting from the indefatigable efforts of Howard Zahniser, that was reported in the press. A near-final version of the National Wilderness Preservation Act, which he wrote, was introduced on February 11, 1959. And as his voice was a major influencing factor in the setting aside of wilderness areas in New York, New Yorkers, including the Association for the Protection of the Adirondacks and the New York State Conservation Council, voiced their strong support for the national wilderness legislation that finally passed Congress in 1964.

This was the genesis of designated wilderness in the Adirondacks and Catskills, where further activities by state agencies, the legislature, and the governor established more than a million acres of wilderness free from aircraft, jeeps, and other vehicles.

Griffen white water on the East Branch of the Sacandaga River. "We must preserve it [the New York State Forest Preserve] in its wild state, its trees, its rocks, its streams"—New York State Court of Appeals, 1932.

The Making of a Wilderness

In 1920, when I was twelve years old, I came to the Adirondack Mountains. My mother had been ill, and it was thought that a period of time in the mountains would refresh her spirits and restore her health. We were to stay at the home of a mountain guide on the edge of what is now the Siamese Ponds Wilderness. His house stood at about two-thousand-feet elevation near the foot of a lofty mountain, with views to the east revealing mountain range on mountain range to the horizon.

My mother's illness turned out to be a blessing in disguise for all our family. I found myself in the midst of the Adirondacks, a land of towering mountains, great forests, and a people uniquely and refreshingly different from those I had known in the city.

By the second summer, I had ingratiated myself to the guide sufficiently well to get an invitation from him to go on a fishing trip "back o' yonder." We entered the great forest by means of a winding trail which snaked its way through the woods to a lovely glacial lake, to a boat, to an island, and finally to a fully equipped log cabin on the island. On state land! From city streets to the depths of a great wild country replete with deer, bear, beaver, and trout! What an outstanding experience for a young boy.

My several mountaineer friends saw at once that I thrived in this wild country, that I had lots of energy, and that I was a willing packer for their frequent excursions into the back country. By the age of seventeen, because of incredible luck, I had taken a fine antlered buck and a bear. This good fortune resulted in the natives asking me to help guide their hunting parties.

Then my brother and I bought an ancient log cabin and seven

Reprinted from the *Conservationist*, May 1985.

acres of land with a mountain stream. The nearest neighbor to the west was more than ten miles distant.

The lure of this cabin country was irresistible. For years I headed north each weekend. I soon got to know the joy of standing atop some storm-swept mountain peak, or sitting around a campfire at a remote beaver pond where the solitude of wilderness was emphasized by the miles of wild country between us and the cabin, by the haunting cry of a loon, and the mysterious sounds in the night.

This land, I had been told, belongs to the people. It was part of the New York State Forest Preserve and protected by the New York State Constitution. Then it was our land. I decided that I must learn as much as possible about the land and that I would begin a library about the Adirondacks.

I started my search for Adirondack books. The wise, old Albany bookseller, John Skinner, sympathetic to my desire to start a library, had convinced me that my first book on the Adirondacks ought to be one he had—an autographed copy of Verplanck Colvin's 1873 report to the legislature. I paid for it in installments over a period of about a month. I took the book home and soon knew it almost by heart.

I began to understand how Colvin must have felt when he stood atop the remote and trailless Seward Mountain on the morning of October 15, 1870. He and his guide had camped the night before high in the mountains and had witnessed an amazing display of the aurora borealis. He had written that "it shot up from the northwest, and passing over to the east, formed a broad crimson belt overhead; while the whole dome of the heavens was lit with a silvery glory, which flashed and swayed in seeming accord with the eddies of a gale then swirling around the mountain." In Colvin's many writings I found that most basic of all joys—the joy of recognition. When Colvin described the Adirondacks (in his early narratives) as "wilderness everywhere, lake on lake, river on river, mountain on mountain, numberless," I knew he spoke the truth, for I had been there and had experienced the same thing myself. And when he told of his unabashed love of the Adirondacks, it was the same love that I felt for my few wilderness acres.

Colvin's writing made me want to learn as much as possible about the Adirondacks and why he would write such beautiful prose for submission to state agencies. I began to find out more about the mountains and how the New York State Forest Preserve came into existence.

At the close of the American Revolution, the crown lands of Great Britain, confiscated by the provisional government, became the property of New York State. They comprised seven million acres, virtually all of the state north of the Mohawk River to the Canadian border.

The region encompassed primeval wilderness of more than a hundred miles in diameter from its near sea level boundary of rivers and lakes. For more than a century, England and France had struggled for control of these vital waterways but wisely refrained from waging battles in the adjacent wilderness because of its incredibly rough terrain.

A book of maps prepared by British army engineers for use by officers of their North American armies was published in London in 1776. It included a map dated 1775 outlining the region now known as the Adirondacks with only surrounding waters noted, and the rest of the map left blank except for these words:

COUCHSACHRAGE
This country by reason of mountains, swamps,
and drowned lands is impassable and uninhabited.

The lands that the British found to be impassable and uninhabited rose gently and occasionally precipitously from the boundary waters to highlands, which in the central region averaged two thousand feet above the boundary waters. Mountain heights exceeded a mile above the sea. More than thirty rivers and streams radiated from near the region's center outward to all points of the compass, dropping more than a thousand feet in their serpentine courses, replete with innumerable waterfalls, flumes, and gorges. Glaciers of the last ice age, more than a mile in thickness, carved out myriad lakes, many near mountaintops.

Here was a land with thousands of mountains and hills, thousands of lakes and beaver ponds, thousands of miles of rivers and streams, and a half-million acres of wetlands. So rough and untamed was the country that generations of pioneers bypassed it in the early days, going up the Mohawk and Saint Lawrence rivers to gentler and more fertile lands in the west. The four-hundred-mile Erie Canal along the Mohawk River was dug by pick and shovel across the state and paid for by tolls more than a decade before the highest peak of the Adirondacks was discovered by a state geologist in 1837. He named it for his sponsor, Governor William Marcy, and christened the range of which it is a part, "the Adirondack group," commemorating an Indian tribe that hunted there.

Hunters and trappers began penetration of the wilderness by canoeing and portaging up its innumerable rivers to remote lakes in the interior. There they built log cabins from the limitless spruce forest and made small clearings to help sustain themselves and their pioneer families.

Wildlife was abundant. A large beaver population had, since ancient times, been building dams on tributary streams, creating ponds and sunlit clearings the length and breadth of the wilderness. Such openings favored a variety of plants and shrubs, which would not grow in an otherwise unbroken forest. The white-tailed deer, moose, bear, marten, fisher, otter, and other animals found ideal habitat there. The mountain lion and wolves were part of the scene. All manner of birdlife, including eagles, hawks, owls, heron, loons, and ducks were common. The crystal streams were alive with trout, and deep, cold lakes had lake trout and whitefish. Salmon were common in the larger lakes and rivers.

Stories of the great forests soon reached receptive ears of people downstate. White pines, six feet in diameter and two hundred feet tall, and great tracts of spruce brought in the enterprising frontiersmen. Soon log bunk houses were filled with lumberjacks who worked long hours and gloried in their ability to cut more trees in a day than their fellows. The lumbermen used horses and oxen to move the logs from the forests to rivers where they floated downstream to mills.

Of the forest composition, spruce and balsam usually dominated the lowlands, around lakes and along rivers and streams. They also crowned most of the several thousand mountains. Giant hardwoods, notably maple and yellow birch, clothed the ridges and mountainsides up to about the three-thousand-foot elevation. Interspersed throughout the forests were giant pines and hemlocks. Cedar and tamarack were common in wetland regions.

The state government, incredibly, by 1870 had deeded away all but forty thousand of the seven million acres of this magnificent country to loggers and private interest groups. Their activities, completely uncontrolled, were transforming rich, lush river valleys into endless miles of dead trees and stumps. Critically important watershed forests on steep mountain slopes were devastated. Forest fires ravaged the mountains, burning the centuries-old forest floor down to bed rock. Rivers and streams began to dry up.

I began to understand through Colvin's writing that he had the vision to see what was happening to the Adirondacks and the courage to do something about it. At the age of twenty-one, he had authored an excellent treatise on the Helderberg Mountains near Albany and a dramatic account of his barometrical measurement of Seward Mountain in the heart of the Adirondacks. By 1872 the legislature had appointed him chief of the Adirondack Topographical Survey and made him a commissioner of State Parks. His first topographical report to the legislature included his discovery of a tiny sheet of water high on the flanks of Mount Marcy, the ultimate source of the Hudson River. He described it as a "tear of the clouds." His report began with these words:

> Since the completion of the primary geological survey of New York there has not been even an attempt at an exploration of the whole of the vast forest now known as the Adirondack Wilderness. For almost all of the exact knowledge that we possess of the topography and physical character of the region, we are indebted to Prof. Emmons and those who so ably assisted him. Through them we first learned that Whiteface Mountain, beforetime placed at about two and a half thousand feet above the sea, and consequently, supposed to be far inferior in altitude to the Catskills, really overtopped, by more than a thousand feet, those more famous and familiar mountains, while southward, towering amidst the clouds, arose a sea of summits grander and still more magnificent.

Serving with Colvin on the State Parks Commission was historian-scientist Franklin B. Hough, former Governor Horatio Seymour, and other distinguished citizens. The commission's first report to the legislature, also submitted in 1873 and obviously written by Colvin, called for the immediate protection of a region comprising 1,730,000 acres of the wild lands in the Adirondacks.

In the following years, Colvin worked tirelessly. With scores of guides, surveyors, axmen, and packers, by horse and wagon and by boat, his expeditions laced the wilderness, then almost entirely privately owned and being pillaged. The lumbermen seemed to have no thought for the future as they cut virgin headwater forests and left them ripe for devastating forest fires, which were certain to come. Dam builders, storing water to flush logs downstream and generate power for their mills, were drowning out lush, verdant river valleys and creating a desolation for wildlife. Colvin's published reports were being read by a growing number of people concerned with the protection as well as the exploitation of the mountains.

In 1885 the recommendations of Colvin and Hough finally took form when the committee headed by Charles Sargent successfully espoused the "forever wild" statute that created the New York State Forest Preserve of lands in the Adirondacks and Catskills. The amount of land had increased to 681,000 acres, much of which had reverted back to the state for unpaid taxes. The "forever wild" statute was incorporated into law to be administered by a forest commission established a year earlier.

Public attention had become focused on the mountain regions of the state. The creation of the Adirondack Park in 1892, which included 2.8 million acres of both public and private lands in the Adirondacks, gave substance to the "forever wild" statute.

Because the Forest Commission was failing in its administration of the forest preserve, leading citizens and statesmen sought to find a way to permanently protect the watershed forests. The unanimous approval of a "forever wild" covenant by the Constitutional Convention of 1894 stripped the Forest Commission of its control of the forest preserve and put it in the hands of the people. The most potent argument advanced for its approval was the protection of the critically important watershed forests. Three of the five members of the convention's Committee on Forest Preservation were delegates from the Adirondacks who were witnessing the rivers in drought and flood. Colvin's description of these forests, which he reprinted numerous times in his reports, had echoed down through the years. He wrote after his 1870 ascent of Seward Mountain:

> The Adirondack wilderness contains the springs, which are the sources of our principal rivers and canals. Each summer the water supply for these rivers and canals is lessened, and commerce has suffered. The immediate cause has been the chopping and burning off of vast tracts of forest in the wilderness, which have hitherto sheltered from the sun's heat and evaporation the deep and lingering snows, the brooks and rivulets, and the thick, soaking sphagnous moss which, at times knee deep, half water and half plant, forms hanging lakes upon the mountainsides, throwing out constantly a chilly atmosphere, which condenses to clouds the warm vapor of the winds, and still reacting, resolves them to rain. With the destruction of the forests, these mosses dry, wither and disappear, with them vanishes the cold, condensing atmosphere which forms the clouds. Now the winter snows accumulate on the mountains, unprotected from the sun, melt suddenly and rush down laden with disaster.

Colvin's writings emphasized the unique and vital values of a protected watershed and other natural resources. It was clear that he understood the inspirational value that they might be to people. But, I soon learned that many did not share Colvin's view and that numerous attacks on the "forever wild" clause were made by various interests wanting to exploit the forest preserve's resources. Mile after mile of land denuded of forest, beset with numerous fires, streams choked with silt and debris, an absence of fish and wildlife—all attested to that fact. I began to realize that the historic legislation, of which Colvin was so much a part, did not secure wilderness preservation. State holdings were too meager and too scattered to provide protection for the remaining wilderness, largely privately owned, that were being ripped and torn asunder! I became convinced that I must—in some small way—help preserve this wonderful country. It was Colvin's vision that served as my first inspiration.

Gradually state acquisitions filled in voids in state holdings. Often lands were stripped of their forests and in devastated condition, when the state regained what it had practically given away. It would require generations of natural processes to restore these lands to a semblance of their former beauty.

As the size of the forest preserve increased in both the Adirondacks and Catskills and the dreams of Colvin and Hough began to be realized, the people of the state began to see the potential for great mountain parks. A strong constituency began to develop as visionary statesmen and leaders of major conservation groups supported legislative actions that increased both the size of the parks and the forest preserve. In 1901 the Association for the Protection of the Adirondacks was organized by an acting lieutenant governor whose initial purpose was to block the state from lumbering 100,000 acres of virgin forest in the Raquette Lake region. Its membership soon included many of the large landowners in the Adirondacks who perceived the forest preserve to be essential to the integrity of a magnificent region. Members included the eminent lawyer Louis Marshall and others who were to devote their lives and their fortunes to the protection of the forest preserve. The association became the legislative watchdog for the forest preserve. By 1916 the forest preserve in the Adirondacks contained 1,765,000 acres. Bond issues of 1916 and 1926 soon added another 638,000 acres including 128,000 acres of virgin forest. By 1931 the Adirondack Park, whose boundary encompassed the majority of forest preserve land along with important scattered private holdings, had doubled in size. Yet there still was no designated wilderness.

Through my scouting and then through membership on a hiking club's conservation committee, I was led step by step in 1931 to the home of John S. Apperson, an official of the General Electric Company. He was, I was told, the preeminent conservationist of our region, a Virginian who had climbed Mount Marcy on skis in 1912 and who, from that experience, had decided to devote his life to the support of the "forever wild" covenant in the constitution. My association with Mr. Apperson began what has turned out to be a lifelong involvement and commitment to the integrity of the forest preserve.

Apperson was at the time in the middle of a battle against a proposal that would permit the state to reforest and commercially lumber its lands outside the boundaries of the Adirondack and Catskill parks. At the time, places like Lake George, Schroon Lake, Lake Champlain, and Sacandaga Reservoir were outside the "blue line," the term that defined the boundary of the Adirondack Park. He felt these scenic regions were essential for a well-balanced park. Former Governor Alfred E. Smith and Senator Ellwood Rabenold, president of the New York State Fish, Game, and Forest League, were Apperson's enthusiastic supporters. Apperson's group produced pamphlets, gave speeches and produced a documentary movie to help their cause. However, Governor Franklin D. Roosevelt and scores of major organizations, including the Association for the Protection of the Adirondacks, and state agencies were in favor of the proposal. The electorate approved it.

A remarkable event took place as a result of the controversy. To reduce opposition to the amendment, legislation was introduced to bring into the park the many threatened border regions. As a result, the legislature added 1.5 million acres to the Adirondack Park. What appeared to be a defeat resulted in a great victory.

My joy was soon tempered by knowledge that a devastating amendment to the "forever wild" clause had passed two legislatures and was to come before the electorate in 1932. The proposal would permit the legislature to authorize the construction of buildings and appurtenances anywhere in the forest preserve. The effect of this so-called closed cabin amendment would be to return control of the forest preserve to the legislature where it had been vested forty years before with disastrous results. The amendment was, in part, a reaction to a Court of Appeals decision in 1930 banning the state from constructing an Olympic bobsled run at Lake Placid. This action, successfully argued in the courts by the Association for the Protection of the Adirondacks, became the legal cornerstone for all subsequent challenges to the integrity of the preserve.

The closed cabin amendment posed an ultimate threat to future wilderness. Our group, led by Apperson, moved to alert people all

John S. Apperson and his disciple Paul Schaefer, 1947. "I was led step by step to John S. Apperson, who had years earlier decided to devote his life to support the 'forever wild' constitutional covenant"—Paul Schaefer. Photograph by Howard Zahniser, by permission of Alice B. Zahniser.

across the state. The Association for the Protection of the Adirondacks formed a statewide committee to fight its passage. Included on the committee were representatives from the Adirondack Mountain Club, the Izaak Walton League, and other concerned citizens, including myself. It had to be an all-out effort. The proposal had been introduced by Adirondack legislators who refused to debate the issue. Once again the strategy was a wide distribution of pamphlets, innumerable letters, articles in state and national magazines and a documentary film, *Our Wilderness?*

This issue brought me in personal contact with many statesmen and citizen leaders, including the trustees of the Association for the Protection of the Adirondacks and Russell Carson of the Adirondack Mountain Club. It was my introduction to the political process and how public opinion could pressure the legislature.

During the fight, Apperson sent a friend and me to film a forest fire near Tahawus and vistas atop Mount Marcy. One of Apperson's cardinal rules was that you had to stand on the ground of any land in question before you could accurately discuss it. We had just set the tripod on the summit when Bob Marshall and his guide Herb Clark appeared. Marshall, the son of Louis Marshall, was at the peak of his career as an explorer, mountaineer, and author. It was July 15, 1932. Bob had just returned from the Arctic. Unfamiliar with the critical Adirondack issues at hand, he was dumbfounded to learn of the closed cabin amendment and very upset when we pointed to the lumbering of virgin forest on Mount Adams six miles distant and the fire scars on North River Mountain. We photographed Herb Clark while Bob was circling the summit, his hair blowing wildly in the wind. Then he came over and said with a determination I shall never forget: "We simply must band together—all of us who love the wilderness. We must fight together—wherever and whenever wilderness is attacked. We must mobilize all of our resources, all of our energies, all our devotion to wilderness. To fail to do this is to permit the American wilderness to be destroyed."

Marshall promised aid from Washington, and he delivered it in articles and speeches until the battle was over. The closed cabin amendment was defeated by a plurality of over six hundred thousand votes, much of it coming from New York City where Senator Rabenold had worked so diligently. We felt that we had survived the baptism of fire, and the enthusiasm we experienced as a result of that victory would last for years, as would our reliance on the scores of friends we had made across the state.

But the establishment of wilderness areas protected from human intrusions was still years away. I was disturbed at Bob Marshall's remark that "the universe of the wilderness, all over the United States, is vanishing with appalling rapidity. It is melting away like the last snowbank on some south-facing mountainside during a hot afternoon in June."

After Marshall organized the Wilderness Society, I was named to one of its committees at the first New York City meeting. And I was moved at his description of wilderness:

> It is the song of the hermit thrush at twilight and the lapping of the waves against the shoreline and the melody of the wind in the trees. It is the unique odor of balsams and of freshly turned humus and of mist rising from mountain meadows. It is the feel of spruce needles under foot and sunshine in your face and wind blowing through your hair. It is all of these at the same time, blended into a unity that can only be appreciated with leisure and which is ruined with artificiality.

One of the most significant actions in support of the "forever wild" covenant occurred when the Constitutional Convention of 1938 reiterated the law, merely changing its number in the New York State Constitution from Article VII, Section 7, to Article XIV, Section 1. Honorable O. Byron Brewster, as chairman of the convention's Conservation Committee, heard all the arguments pro and con. An overwhelming majority of delegates, urged by the solid preservationist constituency, affirmed the law without change in its basic declaration.

During the next few years, the then conservation department was filling in voids in state ownership of remote regions, and gradually our dreams of a better protected wilderness began to take shape. National attention was focused on World War II and assaults on the forest preserve quieted.

But the problems were not over. The close of the war brought renewed emphasis on power production. A massive attack on the Moose River country began in 1945 when a dam near Higley Mountain came to the point of imminent construction. On the South Branch of the Moose River and adjacent country were some of the finest stands of virgin forests left in the East. Lovely lakes and streams, the state's largest winter yarding ground for deer, abundant wildlife—all these were to be inundated. We recognized this magnificent region as a frontier that simply could not be breeched without the most dire consequences to the rest of the preserve. Ed Richard and I, along with others, formed the

Adirondack Moose River Committee and began what was to be the largest, longest, and most expensive conservation fight in the country.

Into this scenario in 1946 came Howard Zahniser of the Wilderness Society. He, Ed Richard, and I had packed through Avalanche Pass to the Flowed Lands where we camped in an open lean-to. We had just returned from Hanging Spear Falls on the Opalescent River, had finished our final meal there, when Howard went down to the water's edge, to sit in the sun with his feet in the water. He was looking across the water toward the lofty MacIntyre Mountains and its virgin forest. I joined him. He spoke quietly. "I've been trying to make a comparison of this view with some other one I know," he said, "but there's nothing else I've seen quite like it. It has the same kind of perfection I sensed when looking at the Grand Tetons." Then getting up he looked up the valley toward Mount Colden and Avalanche Pass and said, "So this was Bob Marshall's country. No wonder he loved it so."

One of our conversations on the trip was most significant in light of future events. Zahniser said, "In addition to such protection as national parks and monuments are now given, we need some strong legislation which will be similar in effect on a national scale to what Article XIV, Section 1, is to New York—to reclaim for the people, perhaps through their representatives in the Congress, control over the wilderness regions of America."

Zahniser became an eloquent advocate of our cause. In Washington, he mustered national assistance for us on a massive scale not only from conservationists of great stature but editors, labor leaders, and heads of federal agencies. He became a frequent visitor with his family to the Adirondacks where he purchased a mountaineer's cabin not far from the ancient log cabin that my brother and I had bought years before. During the following years, while he and I fought for wilderness, our growing families spent countless summer days hiking and camping together in this cabin country and in the beckoning High Peaks region to the north.

Eighteen years later, thanks largely to Zahniser's dedication and indefatigable spirit, his dream became a reality. On September 3, 1964, four months after Zahniser's death, the President of the United States affixed his signature to the National Wilderness Preservation Act, which automatically protected a little more than nine million acres of the nation's most cherished lands. People across the country finally had a definition of wilderness. In the act, Zahniser had written: "A wilderness, in contrast with those areas where man and his own works dominate the landscape, is hereby recognized as an area where the earth and

Five Ponds Wilderness. "Wilderness . . . an area where earth and its community of life are untrammeled by man"—Howard Zahniser, 1964. NYS Department of Environmental Conservation.

its community of life are untrammeled by man, where man himself is a visitor who does not remain."

Significantly, President Johnson called Zahniser's wife, Alice, to Washington for the signing of the act and then presented her with the pen. At the time, she was at her Adirondack cabin.

Opposition to the dam on the Moose River gained force. In 1947 Assembly Speaker Oswald D. Heck convinced Governor Thomas E. Dewey to halt the Moose River Project. Our joy was short-lived when soon afterward it was announced that a larger dam would be built near Panther Mountain on the same river downstream where more private land was involved.

Several years of legal and political maneuvering ensued. We had just about reached a dead end when Speaker Heck again intervened. He created a Joint Legislative Committee on River Regulation for New York State and charged it to exhaust the Moose River issue. Assemblyman John Ostrander was named chairman. A series of public hearings further alerted the people and the press to the issues. At Buffalo Frank Moore, who was state comptroller, advocated that the section of the 1913 amendment to the constitution authorizing the use of up to 3 percent of forest preserve land for regulating the flow of streams be eliminated. At a hearing in New York City, many federal agencies concerned with natural resources testified against the dam. It was at this point that I began to believe that anything was possible in the Adirondacks—even large wilderness tracts!

By 1953 the electorate had approved a committee recommendation for an amendment to the constitution outlawing all regulating reservoirs except those specifically approved by the legislature and the people. Under this amendment, the proposed Panther dam was approved by the legislature but killed by a plurality of over a million votes. With the defeat of this dam project, thirty other smaller reservoirs located in remote regions of the Adirondacks also went down the drain. It took eleven years and a score of major court and legislative actions to prevent the construction of Higley and then Panther dams.

During this period, the New York State Conservation Council came of age. Led by its founder, Karl T. Frederick, Herman Forster, Donald Tobey, Robert Thompson, Michael Petruska, and others, the council with more than a thousand clubs located in more than fifty counties was decisive in the great successes we achieved in the fight for free-flowing rivers. Cooperating with the Adirondack Moose River Committee and the Conservation Council was a coalition of bird clubs, labor unions, and garden and service clubs. The legislature became acutely aware of the political muscle we now had. Slowly but surely, New York residents were defining what they wanted their forest preserve to be.

Another serious threat to wild country came right after the war when jeeps, half-tracks, and planes became more commonplace. The new mechanized equipment could go almost anywhere a horse could. With such equipment, all the trappings of civilization could find their way into the most remote regions.

The quiet of the wilderness was now echoing to the sound of motors. Assembly Speaker Oswald E. Heck called for the creation of the New York State Joint Legislative Committee on Natural Resources in

1951 and charged it with settling this and some of the other vexing Adirondack problems.

The committee, headed by Senator Wheeler Milmoe for eight years, and then headed by Assemblyman Robert Watson Pomeroy for seven years, met with an advisory group of sixteen members with a wide representation from commercial groups as well as conservationists. I was one of the advisors. It was a vitally active group. We made many trips into both parks and hiked into numerous wilderness regions. After a series of monthly meetings and scores of public hearings, a substantial inventory of the natural resources of both the Adirondacks and Catskills was completed.

The committee also settled the perennial forest preserve land loss question by initiating five legislative acts that stopped the annual loss of hundreds of acres of land and by creating a land bank of four hundred acres of forest preserve to make possible better designed roads on the deteriorated highway system in the park.

In 1956 the question of motorized vehicles came to a head when jeeps penetrated Second Pond Flow, four and one half miles into the Siamese Ponds region. This started a definite movement to close large and important wild areas to mechanized transport.

Conservation Commissioner Sharon J. Mauhs began thinking about such regulations in 1957. He visited both the Siamese Ponds and High Peaks regions. In October of the following year with the approval of Governor Averill Harriman, Mauhs issued a paper entitled "Project Forest Preserve." He closed the Siamese Ponds region to motor vehicles. Coming just before the big-game hunting season, it caused a storm of protest by hunters who were ready to move their heavy camping equipment back into favored areas as they had done for years. The protest was so strong it appeared that the regulation might be canceled, but Adirondack residents provided horse and wagon transportation, and the storm subsided.

Then a whole series of actions began. With the Mauhs action cited as a beginning of protected wilderness regions, the New York State Conservation Department's Division of Lands and Forests advocated a wilderness system. Pomeroy, who had become a senator and had taken over the leadership of the Joint Legislative Committee on Natural Resources, set his staff into motion. He asked Dr. Neil Stout, a forester from Syracuse University, and Clarence Petty, who was then on loan to the Pomeroy Committee by the conservation department, to identify all areas in the forest preserve worthy of wilderness designation. Their work was monumental. They outlined eleven major regions totaling

Sharon Mauhs on Black Mountain. In 1958 Conservation Commissioner Sharon J. Mauhs called for studies of the High Peaks and Siamese Ponds areas. This was the first official step in establishing protected wilderness regions in the Adirondack Forest Preserve.

772,000 acres in the Adirondacks. Their findings were published in the 1960 annual report of the committee.

On February 21, 1961, Pomeroy introduced in the assembly for study purposes an act "to amend the conservation law, in relation to the establishment of wilderness areas in the forest preserve, and to regulate the use thereof." Public hearings were held in Indian Lake, Saranac Lake, Utica, and Kingston. Strong support as well as bitter opposition surfaced. The major worry of preservationists was that by giving special protection to perhaps a million acres of the more than two-million-acre preserve, the protection afforded by the "forever wild" clause would be surrendered. Pomeroy insisted that this was not contemplated.

Meanwhile, certain members of the advisory committee, including

Karl Frederick, Lithgow Osborne, and myself, insisted that the conservation department already had the necessary authority. It was pointed out that in 1958 Commissioner Mauhs, with the approval of the governor, had closed trails into the Siamese Pond wilderness area. A special meeting of Commissioner Harold Wilm's (Mauhs' successor) advisory committee was called on September 14, 1961, to discuss the question. Twenty-nine people were in attendance, and Pomeroy was asked to lead the discussion. Many of us served on Wilm's advisory committee as well as on the Joint Legislative Committee on Natural Resources. After considerable debate, it was determined that the conservation commissioner should request an opinion from the attorney general on three points: (1) Does the commissioner have the authority to ban aircraft in the forest preserve? (2) Does he have the right to ban motor boats there? (3) Does he have the authority to ban motor vehicles thereon?

On December 1, 1961, Attorney General Nathaniel Goldstein assured the commissioner that according to the law he had "care, custody, and control of the forest preserve and that he had the right to regulate the uses thereof." Accordingly Pomeroy withdrew the wilderness bill and canceled the remaining public hearings. He then began to seriously concentrate on the establishment of wilderness areas in both parks. In 1962 he released a brochure advocating an increased number of such areas in the preserve. The decision evoked a strong feeling of relief from those of us who for years had dreamed of a genuinely protected system of wilderness regions.

On April 27, 1965, Commissioner Wilm formally proposed the creation of twelve wilderness tracts in the Adirondacks and four in the Catskills, totaling 882,000 acres. He also approved signs designating such areas as being off limits to mechanization. Sportsmen indicated their approval of the proposal when a vote was taken on a county-by-county basis by the New York State Conservation Council. The vote counted thirty-nine counties favoring such wilderness protection and only two opposing it.

In 1967 two major issues focused public attention on the Adirondack Forest Preserve. First was an amendment to build a dam that would inundate thirty-five miles of the Upper Hudson River near the center of the park. The legislature, reacting to public outcry, reaffirmed that they wanted neither the lands of the forest preserve to be destroyed nor the wild rivers to be dammed. They rejected the proposal unanimously in both the senate and the assembly. They also rejected a proposed Adirondack Mountains National Park that would have taken control of the High Peaks and central lakes regions from the state and placed them with the federal government. Because of the extreme pressure from both sides on both issues, Governor Nelson A. Rockefeller saw the need to establish long-range plans for the Adirondacks and Catskills and created a Temporary Study Commission on the Future of the Adirondacks. In 1968 the governor also created the Temporary State Commission on the Water Supply Needs of Southeastern New York. This blue-ribbon panel in three years rejected construction of any storage reservoirs for metropolitan water supply by finding other viable solutions.

The Temporary Study Commission on the Future of the Adirondacks initially was chaired by Leo O'Brien and then by the inimitable Harold Hochschild. Harold A. Jerry, Jr., then director of state planning, became the commission's executive director. They were assisted by an excellent staff and thirty-nine advisors representing a broad spectrum of interests. Again, I was asked to serve as an advisor.

Chairman Hochschild submitted his final report to the governor on December 15, 1970, which was one hundred years to the month after Colvin finished preparing his report on Seward Mountain. It contained 181 specific recommendations and was clearly the finest and most comprehensive report of its kind ever made in New York. Five of the most significant recommendations were:

> Create an Adirondack Park Agency to plan use of all lands, both public and private, in the six-million-acre park;
> Establish a system of wilderness regions where all mechanized travel would be banned;
> Create a Wild, Scenic, and Recreational Rivers system to maintain natural conditions on a thousand miles of rivers;
> Adequately finance a stepped-up land acquisition program;
> Organize an Adirondack Conservancy in the private sector to assist in land acquisitions.

Legislative action soon created the Adirondack Park Agency and the governor appointed Richard W. Lawrence, Jr., as its first chairman. George D. Davis became director of planning. After many hearings were held across the state, the agency prepared a state land master plan. The plan classified about 45 percent of the forest preserve as "wilderness." It designated sixteen wilderness regions, based in part on the earlier work of Stout and Petty, that included about a million acres of the most desirable lands in the forest preserve. In the Catskills four tracts

The signing of the historic Private Land Zoning Act by Governor Nelson Rockefeller with Senator Bernard Smith *(right)*, Assembly Speaker Perry Duryea *(center)*, and Richard Lawrence, Jr., chairman of the Adirondack Park Agency *(left)*, May 22, 1973. © photograph courtesy of the Association for the Protection of the Adirondacks.

containing ninety-two thousand acres were designated by the Conservation Department.

With the specific boundaries of wilderness areas established, Commissioner Henry Diamond, on June 21, 1973, ordered seven hundred lakes closed to aircraft and motor boats. His order listed the lakes by name and location. In his statement he said: "One of the rarest, hence most valuable recreational assets is solitude—a chance to get away from the sight and sound of others. We want to provide areas in which the intrusions of man are minimal. In these, the sound of aircraft and boat motors are an unwelcome reminder of the day-to-day world the visitor is trying to forget."

Commissioner Diamond's order was immediately challenged in the supreme court by owners of an air service, which had been flying into remote areas for years. On November 14, 1973, Justice Edmund Shea rejected the challenge. At last there was legally designated wilderness in the Adirondacks.

One hundred years had elapsed between Verplanck Colvin, Franklin B. Hough, and the State Parks Commission's call for protection of the wild lands in the Adirondacks and the New York State Supreme Court decision that tested the legality of Commissioner Diamond's regulation. The decision was gratifying to countless individuals like myself who, through successive generations, had voiced their plea and had worked tirelessly for the preservation of wilderness in the Adirondack and Catskill mountains.

I have loved this land from the first time I set eyes on it back in 1920. I am happy that I was able to help, along with countless others, to secure wilderness in the forest preserve where generations yet to come can stand, as I have, on a storm-swept mountain peak or sit around a campfire and hear the haunting cry of a loon or the roar of a wild river in an area where the earth and its community of life are untrammeled by man.

2

Rivers, Mountains, Forests

Bouquet River. Free-flowing rivers and streams are the lifeblood of the Adirondacks, and protection of their critical watershed mountains is fundamental. There is no comparable river system in North America.

These essays came about as a result of my growing conviction that free-flowing rivers and streams were the lifeblood of the Adirondacks and that protection of their critical watershed forests was fundamental to their splendor and multiple uses.

Protection of watershed forests was the key philosophy of John S. Apperson. He fought ceaselessly for state acquisition of critical mountain slopes, and with the secretary of the Conservation Commission, Warwick Carpenter, and others, he succeeded in getting important High Peaks areas under the constitutional covenant protecting them. These actions took place from 1915 to 1930, and the lawyer Louis Marshall was involved with them until his death in 1929.

By 1930 many of the nation's leading conservationists became attracted to Apperson's work, which he was dramatizing with photographs of the result of lumbering and fire on many of the Adirondack peaks and the erosion of islands in Lake George. One of these men was Hugh Hammond Bennett of the United States Soil Conservation Service and two of his staff, Dr. John Lamb of Cornell University and Dr. Hugh Wilson of Syracuse University. Dr. Wilson verified for me that it would take from five to ten hundred years for an inch of soil to accumulate on the burned slopes of Black Mountain on the Sacandaga watershed.

Later, Dr. Bernard Frank, assistant chief of the United States Forest Service, reinforced these viewpoints as we walked through the virgin forest in the Ausable Lakes country. "If I had my way," he said, as we observed not only the magnificent trees but also the characteristic thin, fragile soil so evident on the mountain slopes, "I would insist that every forester before getting his degree would see what you and I have seen here today."

One October day, I had lunch with Sigurd Olson, a major proponent of the Quetico-Superior Wilderness Canoe Region, and several members of the Wilderness Society along the surging West Branch of the Sacandaga River in the Silver Lake Wilderness. The day before, we had stood on a high ledge of Crane Mountain looking southwesterly some thirty miles to this region. Olson had asked if it would be possible to have a quick look at one of the Adirondack wilderness regions, so we took off the first thing that morning and drove down along the East Branch of the Sacandaga River to the Piseco Trail which coursed along the West Branch. The stillness of the wilderness was broken only by the music of the rapids and a steady rain, which dripped from the great trees and dappled the running waters. A short distance upstream, the river came out of a deep gorge and foamed over giant boulders to a pool below. Above the gorge, I explained to the group, the river coursed through miles of unbroken forest and other flumes and falls. Sig remarked: "To me this is a perfect river—not too big and not too small. To follow it to its source would be a great adventure."

Before he left for the Quetico-Superior country, I asked him if he would give me his impressions of the rivers of the Adirondacks for use in a documentary film we were producing in support of the Wild, Scenic, and Recreational Rivers System Act, then being debated in the state legislature. Within a short time, he responded with the following, entitled "What a River Means to Me":

A wild river is the life blood of the land. Beginning in mist and rain and snow, its millions of tiny trickles and seepages move downward through duff, humus, and mazes of tangled roots, escaping at times to flow freely over moss and lichen-grown ledges. It gathers to itself many flowages and the little creeks they form, emerging at last as a river on its way to the sea.

In any river of the Adirondacks I see the rivers I've known all over the United States and the great brawling ones of the north as far as the Arctic tundras. When I hear the thunder of a rapids or the soft music of some chuckling stream, when I see placid pools and the widening circles of a rising trout or hear the lonely song of a whitethroat at dusk, I am content and strongly fulfilled, for mine is the blood and the sinew of ancestral man, and within me are memories of forbearers who for countless millennia watched and listened before me. Rivers were part of their lives. They were the highways. Here they hunted and fished, built shelters, and in the glow of campfires had visions and dreams.

The Adirondacks with their magnificent mountain complexes are interlaced by the network of living rivers that shaped them and carved their valleys, rivers as much a part of them as their exposed cliffs and ledges. Only if they are included in the great concept of keeping the Adirondacks "forever wild" can these beautiful mountains fulfill their destiny as refuges for the spirit of man.

This documentary film, which was shown nationwide, had a tremendous impact upon the success of the Wild, Scenic, and Recreational Rivers System Act, which now protects more than a thousand miles of free-flowing Adirondack rivers.

Upper Hudson River Gorge. New York State has established a Wild, Scenic, and Recreational River System to protect over a thousand miles of our rivers, an accomplishment that a few years ago would have seemed impossible. Photograph courtesy of NYS Department of Environmental Conservation.

Wild Rivers

Adirondack rivers always intrigue me, but full appreciation of their splendor and variety came only after years of fighting for their preservation with scores of associates.

I vividly recall a first trip into the Higley Mountain country in May 1945. Here, a dozen miles back in the woods, an unnecessary impoundment threatened to inundate the famous Moose River Plains, the Beaver Lake region and the Indian River.

Although I had backpacked a lot of Adirondack country, the quality of this wilderness surpassed any that I had yet seen. The plains had solitude and Beaver Lake was surrounded with virgin white pines of great beauty. Wildlife was abundant. On the first day, I stood at the shore of Beaver Lake, several deer were feeding on the opposite shore, a bald eagle soared over it, and just about dusk a raccoon made its way along a sandbar. That night we listened to the call of a loon, and later as we were catching bullheads of prodigious size near the east shore, a fearless beaver splashed the waters nearby.

Next morning I followed the outlet of Beaver Lake to Indian River and took a well-worn game trail upstream under ancient pines, which guard it. The crystal-clear water was singing as it sparkled over boulders on its way to join the South Branch of the Moose River, just below the cliffs of Higley Mountain. Above a small rapids, I came upon a long, quiet and still water, its banks bedecked with wildflowers, ferns, and grasses. Immense spruces formed an evergreen canyon upstream, with an occasional pine towering high above their spired tops.

I stood there in awe at the perfection of nature around me. Then came the sudden realization that all of this might soon be lost forever: the great forest reduced to a cemetery of stumps, the rich, lush forest

Reprinted from the *Conservationist*, June–July 1973.

floor alternately drowned and dry; and the music of the river stilled. Even as I stood silent on this spot, a deer emerged from the shadows of the forest to drink in a sunlit pool. Just upstream, a trout leapt for a fly.

Here was wilderness—solitude, serenity, and peace!

Who, having known such moments, could abandon such country to the fate we foresaw?

Years of intense activity followed, during which virtually all outdoor organizations gradually mobilized their forces for the first time in the effort to preserve these irreplaceable lowlands. It took eleven years to assure the preservation of the valley of the South Branch of the Moose River.

A special investigating commission named by Governor Thomas E. Dewey killed the proposed Higley dam in 1947. Shortly thereafter, an even larger reservoir, the Panther Mountain, was proposed for a site about five miles below the proposed Higley Dam on the same river. This issue was the subject of litigation in state and federal courts for several years. An act of the legislature in 1950 banned any dam on the Moose River, and constitutional amendments in 1953 and in 1955 made the issue final.

The record will show that all during this long and exhaustive effort, conservationists offered alternatives to the destruction of this valley. They favored the proposed downstream flood control reservoirs at Forestport and Hawkinsville. They strongly supported the Saint Lawrence River and Niagara Falls power development.

Subsequently other major reservoir proposals surfaced: the Salmon River, the Hudson at Luzerne, and most incredible of all, the Hudson at Kettle Mountain or at a site near the Gooley cabin during the mid-1960s. The latter would have destroyed sixteen thousand acres of prime forest, lake, and river country, the town of Newcomb, the Huntington Wildlife Research Forest, and more. Because the people of our state demonstrated that they cared enough, the legislature and the governor heard their voices clearly; and the projects were shelved. In the case of the proposed Gooley dam, the legislature unanimously adopted legislation to prohibit it, and Governor Rockefeller signed it.

It was only natural, therefore, that when Governor Rockefeller's Temporary Study Commission on the Future of the Adirondacks proposed a Wild, Scenic, and Recreational Rivers System to prevent such destruction, it won overwhelming support. Related to this proposal was the decision of the Association for the Protection of the Adirondacks to create a documentary film on the subject. We felt the public needed an-

Fred Sullivan films the West River Gorge. Adirondack rivers have always intrigued me, but full appreciation of them came only after years of fighting for their preservation.

swers to these basic questions: Where were these rivers? What portions of them would be preserved? And why?

By happy coincidence, a young man from Glens Falls, needing a documentary to get his master's degree in filmmaking from Boston University appeared at our office. Fred Sullivan began his work in April 1971 and completed the film in October 1972.

Guided at times by members of the Adirondack Hudson River Association, but largely on his own, Sullivan and his crew from the university ranged the park, exploring its remote rivers and climbing cataracts to find their sources in high sphagnum swamps and mountaintop lakes. He quickly found the relationship between clouds, trees, and soil; brought wildlife into his viewfinder; and caught the elusive spirit of wilderness campfires on his film. Thunderstorms, black flies, and snowstorms were part of the story. He related the erosion of fragile resources to people in such a way that the need for better planning and controls became obvious.

Starting out with no preconceptions as to Adirondack problems, his thesis crystallized the philosophy expressed by the Adirondack Study Commission. It clearly pointed the way for comprehensive action by all facets of our society. The film spurred action on a problem that will require years to solve completely.

The first major step in this direction was made in 1972 by Assemblyman Glenn H. Harris and State Senator Bernard C. Smith. Their bill, which was passed and signed by the governor, set up a Wild, Scenic, and Recreational Rivers System as was proposed. One hundred and eighty miles of the most critical rivers were included in it, and they now have this special protection.

The Harris-Smith Bill also provided that the Adironack Park Agency, after consultation and cooperation with the environmental conservation commissioner with respect to rivers elsewhere, consider and make proposals to the legislature within three years for the addition of sections of other rivers.

Of the two thousand miles of rivers within the park, a total of about one thousand were to be studied for inclusion in the system. Of this mileage, 180 miles are now in the system. [By 1986, another 1,238 miles of Adironack rivers were brought under the system.] A large percentage of the rivers to be studied are in private ownership where it will be necessary either to purchase or obtain covenants from the owners. Undoubtedly the covenant will be the most viable method of getting protection.

Here is a unique opportunity to give proper consideration to the

Lovely still waters of the Saint Regis River.

northwestern portion of the park where there are tremendous natural resources that have been almost completely overlooked by conservationists.

The principle of a system to protect our rivers has now been fully established—an accomplishment that only a few years ago seemed impossible. It is now up to us to see that this program moves ahead.

We need to develop a rivers ethic that will go beyond legislative or state agency mandates. This ethic should be based on a comprehensive knowledge of the total river resource. Few have this knowledge. It also involves appreciation and understanding of the vast network of tributary streams, scores of which are neither named nor designated on any map. The ethic would be the belief that each of us is custodian of the rivers to their ultimate sources and that we exercise concern for their preservation.

If we will, we could bequeath to posterity a rich heritage of clean, free-flowing rivers and streams, with countless waterfalls and cataracts, and white-water rapids to challenge one's skill. If we do, decades hence many youths will walk down winding mountain trails and will hear, as we have heard, the roar of a distant Adirondack river. Their steps will quicken and they will know strange, new emotions. And that night, before their campfire they will experience, as we have, the unsurpassed exhilaration that only a wild, untamed river can provide.

Watershed Forests

The most fragile and valuable natural resources in the Adirondack Park are the forests that protect the sources of the rivers, which radiate from its heartland outward to all points of the compass. From sphagnous bogs and ledges on the highest peaks, tiny springs and rivulets become splashing cataracts and join the vast network of thirty thousand miles of pure waters that roar through white-water rifts and flumes and canyons, or idle through extensive evergreen forests and wetlands where still waters reflect ferns and flowers of the wilderness and a deer or lynx pauses to drink.

The litany of rivers is as extensive as their names are colorful. The Raquette, the Cedar, the Oswegatchie, the Salmon, the Sacandaga, the Bog, the Beaver, the Independence, the Hudson, the Grass, the Ausable, the West Canada, the Bouquet, the Saint Regis, the Black—these are a few of the rivers, no two alike, which thread like quicksilver between the labyrinth of mountains. This combination of rivers, lakes, mountains, and forests is unique on this planet.

Verplanck Colvin saw this wealth of natural resource and began his crusade for the creation of an Adirondack Park when he was a young man in 1868. Several years later, as a member of a special commission to study the creation of an Adirondack Park, he found that the state lands within the Adirondacks had been decreased, through sales beginning at a few cents an acre, from millions of acres to a paltry forty thousand acres.

The New York State Forest Preserve was created in 1885, and a Forest Commission was appointed to administer its 681,000 acres. The results of this administration were dismal, to say the least, and by the time the Constitutional Convention of 1894 convened, mismanagement

Reprinted from the *Conservationist*, March–April 1977.

Virgin forest at Indian River. The most fragile and valuable resource of the forest preserve is the natural wild forests, which protect the sources of our rivers.

had reached so serious a state that the way was paved for direct constitutional action by the convention.

Colonel David McClure of New York City was appointed chairman of the convention's special committee on Forest Preservation. Three of this five-man committee were official delegates from the Adirondack counties of Essex, Franklin, and Saint Lawrence. The nucleus of their proposal was the statute of 1885 which created the forest preserve. The New York Board of Trade and Transportation gave much thought and inspiration to the problem of insuring the protection of the watershed forests involved.

On August 23, 1894, Mr. McClure reported to the constitutional convention:

> Your committee has had presented to it many valuable arguments and statements bearing on the matter [of forest preservation] and after careful consideration, has unanimously reached the conclusion that it is necessary for the health, safety, and general advantage of the people of the state of New York that the forest lands now owned or hereafter acquired by the State, and the timber on such lands, should be preserved intact as forest preserves, and not under any circumstances be sold.

The records of that constitutional convention clearly show that the preservation of watershed forests in the Adirondacks was the primary issue. Many of the delegates to the convention were from the region involved, and there is no record other than strong support for the covenant unanimously approved by a vote of 144-0 on September 13, 1894. It read as follows: "The lands of the state, now owned or hereafter acquired, constituting the forest preserve as now fixed by law, shall be forever kept as wild forest lands. They shall not be leased, sold, or exchanged, or be taken by any corporation public or private, nor shall the timber thereon be sold, removed, or destroyed."

By 1903 strong public support for the new constitutional covenant had almost doubled the forest preserve in size to 1,305,000 acres.

Then, in that same year, a serious drought hit the park and the worst fears of all who sought protection for the watershed forests came to be. Lumbering had continued unabated on private lands throughout the park including some of the invaluable watershed high peaks. The mountains were ripe for devastating forest fires. That year 464,000 acres burned. Similar conditions prevailed in 1908, despite continued

Forest fire destruction on Wolf Mountain. Wolf Mountain . . .

land acquisition, and another 368,000 acres were devastated. The stark reality of the warnings of the early statesmen became evident, and the state belatedly began to face up to the problem.

Sadly many great Adirondack peaks, and scores of lesser ones, have known the scourge of fires that consumed the soil to bedrock. Today they are stark reminders of lost resources of incalculable value. The great spruce, pine, and hemlock forests of Giant Mountain, Rocky Peak Ridge, Round, Dix, Black, Wolf, Graves, and many more mountains are gone and will not return for thousands of years. The streams that the mountain peaks fed now alternate in flood and low water because of the loss of the vital forests that once stablized their flow.

The lesson we must still learn from such monumental losses is that we must complete the task of protecting watershed forests in the Adirondacks wherever they are!

To understand the unique forest and soil conditions in the park one might well observe a mountain at about four-thousand-feet elevation where a natural slide, triggered by lost forest and overburden of moisture, has occurred. Here you will see the naked rock exposed to the elements. You can observe the thin carpet of soil—often a foot or less in depth—which clings to the once molten rock at precipitous angles and with sliding characteristics. There is no deep mineral soil here, nor

where the stark reality of the warnings of the early statesmen became evident.

sedimentary rocks laid down in flat ledges, which would have a tendency to hold soil and encourage tree growth.

The soil on the mountain slopes is composed for the most part of decayed leaves, tree branches, and fallen trees, and it is often covered with sphagnum mosses and other plants. This soil is held together by intertwining tree roots, a fragile combination that has nevertheless sustained great trees, notably spruce, on most Adirondack mountains except those with alpine conditions above timberline or those that have burned.

On lower elevations, the soil is deeper and there is less danger of forest fires or erosion. Such forests gradually reach maturity, and it is then that they reach their maximum value as regulators of stream flow. Every leaf and tree that falls enriches and deepens the soil base as fungus and mosses assist in their decomposition.

Forest fires often consume the soil to bedrock. When that happens, the watershed forest that heretofore held in check the rain and snow and fed the springs that sustained streams and rivers is lost, and melting snow and rain run unchecked into the valleys below leaving devastating erosion in their wake.

Rich organic topsoil such as that found in the wild forests of the Adirondacks is the best river-regulating reservoir we have. The forest floor, composed of decaying wood and vegetation, gives sustenance to sphagnous moss, tiny plants, and seedling trees, all of which combine to become an extraordinarily efficient sponge to hold water. Each square foot of this topsoil in a living forest can absorb more than two gallons of water, and each square mile will hold more than fifty million gallons of water.

The annual records of the conservation department from 1911 through 1965 clearly show that wild forest land, under the protection of the constitution, rarely burns. If fire occurs, it is usually a ground fire only. The really great conflagrations were fed by debris from lumbering operations and the drying out of the forest floor. Such fires, often on remote mountains and fanned by natural updrafts, have been virtually impossible to control.

One autumn day, I climbed Black Mountain, on the East Branch of the Sacandaga River, with Dr. Hugh Wilson, an eminent forester. This mountain, only about twenty-five-hundred feet elevation, was burned in 1908. The south side had lost its soil and numerous frosts had broken thin slabs of the exposed rock. Here and there the stump of a huge pine, charred and weathered, remained in mute witness to the great forest which once was there.

"How long will it take for an inch of soil to form on this mountain under these conditions?" I asked. "And how long will it be before another forest of similar size can establish itself?"

"From five hundred to a thousand years for the soil formation, and more than five thousand years for the forest to reestablish itself," Dr. Wilson replied.

Despite the unique land ownership pattern within the Adirondack Park, it is still possible to give a reasonably accurate picture of such land ownership:

A high percentage of mountains within the park and the adjacent highlands with important watershed values are in the state-owned forest preserve.

Most significant wilderness regions—a million acres— together with a million and a half acres of wild forest land, much of it in large blocks, are in the forest preserve.

Approximately 75 percent of the streams and 50 percent of the lakes are state-owned.

Most of the large river valleys and much shoreline on the larger lakes are privately owned.

A substantial part of the good, deep-soiled, prime forest-growing lowlands remain in private ownership and to a large extent are under forest management practices.

Forest preserve lands, then, comprise about 40 percent of the six-million-acre park. But this percentage is the minimum that should be reserved for the protection of the watershed, and to enhance the quality of the park, it is logical that these lands be rounded out by further acquisitions and easements.

Indian Pass. "The primary uses of the forest preserve are watershed protection and outdoor forest recreation"—Joint Legislative Committee on Natural Resources, 1965.

A fifteen-year exhaustive, in-depth study of the forest preserve by the Joint Legislative Committee on Natural Resources for New York State under the chairmanship of Senator Pomeroy concluded that the "primary uses of the forest preserve are watershed protection and outdoor forest recreation." It recommended strict adherence to Article XIV, Section 1, of the New York State Constitution.

A special governor's Temporary State Commission on the Water Supply Needs of Southeastern New York recently concluded, after three years of study, that the best place to tap the water supply needs for the metropolitan region on the Hudson River was downstream near Hyde Park. Here the great volume of waters from the Adirondacks could, during many months of the year, supply hundreds of millions of gallons of water daily to augment present metropolitan supplies. The proposal, called "flood skimming," has the support of the United States Army Corps of Engineers.

The recent laws setting up a Wild, Scenic, and Recreational Rivers System in the park designated more than 1,200 miles of rivers to be included. These laws assured their natural free-flowing character and the absence of dams and drowned lands in the park. It is often overlooked or forgotten that on or near the outside periphery of this 9,375-square-mile park are many flood control dams, water storage reservoirs, and power plants, commercially using most of the water yielded by the entire mountain system.

State land acquisition policies in recent years have, for the most part, greatly enhanced the forest preserve. Substantial bond issue money has been approved in referendum and soon will be available once more. A high priority should continue to be placed on forest lands with good watershed values.

The idea of scenic easements on private lands within the Adirondack Park has proved to be of great value. The easement at Elk Lake is a shining example of this approach to keeping highly scenic areas in their natural condition.

Should not watershed forest easements now be considered—not on the sole basis of public enjoyment but on the basis of absolute economic necessity?

Should there not be an exhaustive study made now of all remaining watershed forests in the park? Such a study should not be content to use the old formula "above 2,500 feet elevation." Rather let it begin at whatever elevation high watershed values are found. Let it be nonconfiscating in philosophy and as complementary to private interests as possible.

Elk Lake. This is *Adirondack* land!

The great natural resources that comprise the forest preserve and the park as we know it today remain because there was vision a century ago and there were statesmen who made the vision a reality. At no time in Adirondack history have there been more opportunities to enhance the park than exist now. Let us be up and doing!

A Sound of Falling Water

The Adirondack Dome comprises about 13,000 square miles or about 25 percent of the total area of New York State. Roughly the shape of a beaver pelt, this uplift of ancient rock is part of the vast Canadian Shield. The region is essentially a mountain island surrounded by near-sea-level waters. The Saint Lawrence River on the north, Lake Champlain on the east, the Mohawk River on the south, and the Black River on the west are all about one to seven hundred feet above the sea. Waters from mile-high peaks in the northeastern Adirondacks, from more than a thousand lesser mountains, from 2,760 lakes, 30,000 miles of rivers and streams, and 800,000 acres of wetlands feed this vast river system which flows outward from central elevations to all points of the compass.

There is no comparable river system in North America.

Within this geologic Adirondack region is the 9,375-square-mile Adirondack Park, protecting the headwater forests of five great watersheds by constitutional covenant, assuring continued improvement of the watershed, increased stability of stream flow and maximum protection from forest fires. With the mean height of the Adirondack plateau being above two thousand feet in elevation, it follows that the thirty major rivers rising there drop an average of about two thousand feet into the surrounding boundary waters. The inevitable result of so much water flowing so steeply downhill is numberless waterfalls, cascades, flumes, gorges, and white waters.

The original boundaries of the Adirondack Park were located well up on the great plateau, leaving most of the major potential hydroelectric sites just outside the "blue line." Subsequent additions to the park, notably on the south, east, and north, dropped the elevations of the

Reprinted from *Adirondack Life*, September 1980.

West Branch of the Ausable River. A lifetime will not be long enough to complete the Adirondack rivers adventure.

park boundaries, but the westerly segment has remained substantially intact since the Act of 1892 created the park.

I became aware of the great scenic attractions of the rivers that flow through the boundaries of the park several years ago while photographing the rivers for Adirondack documentary films. Not only was I impressed by the great number of waterfalls we found on river after river, I was amazed to find that in those months of the year when they were in maximum splendor, few people enjoy these great river spectacles.

The Adirondack Boundary Rivers Tourway has been designated to make people aware of the great natural beauty to be found around the outside periphery of the Adirondack Park. Best of all, the Tourway requires no new roads, no bridges, no multimillion-dollar program to make it possible: it's all there now, just waiting to be seen and appreciated.

From Albany the circle distance to the thirty staging areas shown on the accompanying map is about six hundred miles. Added to this shortline distance will be about five hundred miles as the various waterfalls, flumes, and gorges are visited. At each staging area or site, people can begin a river adventure.

This is not a journey that can be completed in a week or a month.

Each staging area will afford an adventure in exploring not only the rivers and streams, but the lovely rural and wild country so entrancingly intermixed. Here will be found ancient forts, inns, and firesides, for this boundary rivers country is a historic region, once the battleground of empires that tried to claim it. There is no proliferation of signs, and you will see lots of evidence that people are proud of their countryside. The roads are excellent, the bridges often works of engineering art.

During a major part of the journey the traveler will be within sight of rivers, streams, lakes, reservoirs, or wetlands. Many waterfalls are visible from highways. Others will require short walks for the most outstanding views. You will see scores of hydroelectric stations you never knew existed. Except for those intrigued by an individual river that invites exploration, backpacking is not required.

Except during occasional periods of drought, about four inches of precipitation per month fall on the Adirondacks. Despite this regularity, the stream flow in July, August, and September varies greatly because billions of trees retain incredible amounts of water for making wood during the growing season. The prime period to see the rivers therefore is in April, May, and early June, or after the normal rains in September.

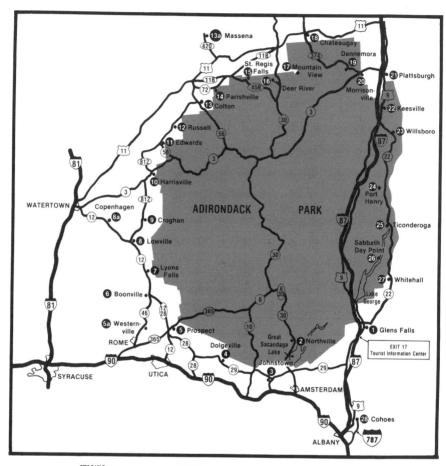

STAGING AREA	RIVER	STAGING AREA	RIVER	STAGING AREA	RIVER
①	Hudson	⑩	Oswegatchie	⑳	Saranac
②	Sacandaga	⑪	Oswegatchie	㉑	Champlain-Valcour
③	Caroga-Mohawk	⑫	Grasse	㉒	Ausable
④	East Canada	⑬	Raquette	㉓	Bouquet
⑤	West Canada	⑬a	St. Lawrence	㉔	Lake Champlain
⑤a	Delta	⑭	St. Regis	㉕	Ticonderoga
⑥	Black	⑮	St. Regis	㉖	Lake George
⑦	Moose	⑯	Deer	㉗	Lake Champlain
⑧	Independence	⑰	Salmon	㉘	Mohawk
⑧a	Deer	⑱	Chateaugay		
⑨	Beaver	⑲	Chazy		

Map of Boundary Rivers Tourway. NYS Department of Environmental Conservation.

Saint Regis River Falls. The Adirondack Nature Conservancy, through its purchases, scenic easements, and sanctuaries, has made it possible for people to hear the sounds of many falling waters.

Winter months find the rivers especially beautiful. But even during low-water periods, the opportunity to explore the geology of the river beds or gorges makes even low water a blessing at times.

A classic example of man's use of a river is found in West Canada Creek. Rising in the west-central West Canada Lakes Wilderness and fed by scores of lakes, the stream is halted by Hinckley dam atop the plateau in the extreme southwestern corner of the park. Millions of gallons of water daily take care of the municipal requirements of Utica; other water is diverted for hydroelectric energy and then becomes the stabilizer of the Barge Canal system in the Mohawk River. On its way down to join the Mohawk, the West Canada courses through a deep canyon about three miles long. It once was considered the rival of Niagara Falls, its charm not less but of a different dimension than Niagara's. It is breathtaking in spring or winter.

To detail all the routes that serve the thirty staging areas would require a book, and it would take away much of the fun of adventuring. It will not be difficult to find falls and gorges near the recommended villages. Indeed the existence of a population center is itself a virtual guarantee that there is a waterfall, gorge, or rapid nearby, for settlements always sprang up near sources of water power for the local mills which formed the first industrial facilities of the area. Nearby residents will be cooperative with information and if requested, some will act as guides. As an example of the attractions to be found, consider staging area 1:

> Proceed up the Adirondack Northway from Albany to about mile 41. Here the highway crosses the Hudson River. Just beyond the river is the Department of Transportation Information Center where a large map of the Tourway will be found. From this center proceed northerly to Exit 18, from which point take the Corinth Road westerly towards the village of Corinth. About seven miles along this road there is a sign on the left-hand side announcing a scenic and picnic area, courtesy of International Paper Company. A walk of a hundred yards or so will bring you to a high bluff overlooking the Hudson River, across which is a large and dramatic dam serving International Paper. Continuing on this road 1.5 miles brings you to the village of Corinth. Here Palmer Falls may be seen, both from a gravel road leading along the north bank of the river and from streets in the village itself. County Route 4 easterly follows the river for several miles before reaching Spier Falls, once one of the largest hydroelectric stations in the world. Below this station, just before the highway turns up the mountain, you will have a fine view of the river heading towards what appears to be an impassable mountain barrier. Returning to Corinth, proceed up state Route 9W to the Hadley House, taking a left fork one mile to a high iron bridge spanning the white waters of the Sacandaga River. Just beyond this bridge is the village of Luzerne. Turn right on County Route 4 to the bridge that crosses the Hudson River just below Luzerne Falls. From the bridge the confluence of the Sacandaga with the Hudson may be seen.

Staging area 2 can be reached by continuing westerly on County Route 4 to Northville, and the others follow in clockwise order around the periphery of the park. The villages in close proximity to major scenic river views are as follows:

2. Northville: Sacandaga River. 3. Johnstown: Caroga- Mo-
hawk River. 4. Dolgeville: East Canada Creek. 5. Prospect:
West Canada Creek. 5a. Westernville: Delta Reservoir. 6.
Boonville: Black River. 7. Lyons Falls: Moose River. 8.
Lowville: Independence River. 8a. Copenhagen: Deer River.
9. Croghan: Beaver River. 10. Harrisville: Oswegatchie
River. 11. Edwards: Oswegatchie River. 12. Russell: Grasse
River. 13. Colton: Raquette River. 13a. Massena: Saint
Lawrence River. 14. Parishville: Saint Regis River. 15. Saint
Regis Falls: Saint Regis River. 16. Deer River: Deer River.
17. Mountainview: Salmon River. 18. Chateaugay: Chateau-
gay River. 19. Dannemora: Chazy River. 20. Morrisonville:
Saranac River. 21. Plattsburgh: Lake Champlain. 22. Keese-
ville: Ausable River. 23. Willsboro: Bouquet River. 24. Port
Henry: Lake Champlain. 25. Ticonderoga: Lake Champlain.
26. Sabbath Day Point: Lake George. 27. Whitehall: Lake
Champlain. 28. Cohoes: Mohawk River (Exit 6 Northway)

A trip around the Adirondack Park will give you an understanding of the region you can get no other way. The term "Adirondack
Dome" used by geologists will become readily understandable, for you
will see foothills rising steadily upward from the Mohawk to the mountains in the distance, an escarpment scores of miles in length rising more
than a thousand feet above the lowlands of the Black River valley. In
the Saint Lawrence valley the escarpment increases gradually in height
easterly to the Champlain valley. From these easterly waters the dome
rises sharply, in hundreds of mountains, culminating in Mount Marcy,
only forty miles inland and just a few feet short of a vertical mile above
the waters of Lake Champlain.

It makes little difference at which staging area you decide to start
exploring. You will find adventure wherever you go. And later on, as
you visit the rivers within the park, you will find in them a new meaning because you understand them in their most dramatic forms along
the boundaries of the park.

Completing this thousand-mile Tourway will produce the same
conviction that many of us now accept—that the Adirondacks will always be a land we will never know completely. There will always be a
mystery about it, for there is too much of it to crowd into a lifetime.

West Canada Gorge. These waters drop in countless falls, cataracts, and gorges.

The Mohawk Valley

HEARTLAND OF THE EMPIRE STATE

A thousand miles of streams, born of crystal springs on remote highlands, combine to form the lovely Mohawk River in central New York State.

These waters drop in countless falls, cataracts, and flumes from elevations more than three thousand feet above the ocean tides, which swell the Hudson River below the great falls of the Mohawk at Cohoes. For countless years, these streams have been carving the crystalline gneiss and sedimentary rocks into land and waterscapes that rival in picturesque beauty anything that might be found in this Empire State.

Clouds brushing the tops of more than thirty storm-scarred mountains in the West Canada Lakes Wilderness in the Adirondack Park leave their tribute of moisture on the rocks, needles, leaves, and trees, where it crystallizes into droplets and soaks into the spongelike mosses and duff. Then it gradually percolates downward in tiny, unseen rivulets to form the ultimate visible sources of the Mohawk River. One of the highest glacial pools to receive this water is Twin Lake, 2,654 feet above the sea. Nearby, the three West Canada lakes above twenty-three-hundred-feet elevation form the main headwaters of the stream by that name. In like manner, scores of deep ravines on Indian Head Mountain high in the Catskill Park are the southern sources of the Schoharie that has tributaries like the Westkill, the Minekill, and many others, which add dramatically to this great watershed. Well over a hundred airline miles separate these high north and south sources of the Mohawk. From the peaks of the West Canada Lakes Wilderness, the Adirondack High Peaks are visible, as are thousands of square miles of wilderness to the north and scores of glacial lakes. From Indian Head in

Reprinted from the *Mohawk Valley* magazine, March–April 1980.

the Catskills, one can look down upon the Hudson River valley nearly halfway between Albany and New York City. In the extreme northwest of the watershed, on the Tug Hill Plateau, the Mohawk has an official beginning, 155 miles from its confluence with the Hudson. On this plateau, as well as in the extreme north and south watershed, precipitation reaches fifty-two inches annually. The Oriskany, the Canajoharie, the East Canada, the Cayadutta, the Plotterkill, and many more streams swell the Mohawk. The great reservoirs at Delta and Hinkley maintain the constant summer flows of the Mohawk.

The Mohawk is the only river that has cut its course through the great uplift of country known as the Appalachian Plateau, which extends from the southern Adirondacks and Maine to Alabama. Generally speaking, the Adirondacks are on the north side of the main valley. They are part of the vast Canadian Shield, the geologic roots of North America, more than a billion years old. At Big Nose Mountain and at Little Falls, west of Amsterdam and Herkimer respectively, the Adirondack rock actually crosses the Mohawk River to meet the much younger Appalachians south of it.

Geologists speculate that the sources of the Mohawk were once east of Little Falls. The Saint Lawrence valley was blocked by a depth of nearly two miles of ice during the last ice age, which retreated about ten thousand years ago. As a result, all the water from the Great Lakes region and southern Canada poured in torrential volumes down the Mohawk. They cut the gorge at Little Falls, dug deep ravines and pot holes, and created the great aquifer at Schenectady, which yields twenty million gallons of pure water a day under the fertile flats near that city. The river then was two miles wide and very deep. Evidences of its power and of the cutting forces of the glacial drift are readily seen all the way downriver to the Hudson.

Hundreds of waterfalls result from the three-thousand foot drop of the high tributary streams to the Hudson at Cohoes. Probably the most famous of these were, in early days, the Great Falls at Cohoes and Trenton Falls on the West Canada. Descriptions of the falls, paintings of them by great artists, and books devoted solely to their extraordinary beauty received worldwide distribution in the late nineteenth century. The need for municipal water supplies, for the regulation of the canal, and for power have diminished but not obliterated the splendor of these places. At times, even today, the volume of water in the Mohawk exceeds the one hundred thousand cubic feet a second which goes over both the American and Canadian portions of Niagara Falls. The Schoharie alone at times exceeds fifty-six thousand cubic feet of water a second at its confluence with the Mohawk.

Many lakes and ponds in the watershed highlands serve as storage reservoirs for later use. Caroga and East Caroga Lakes, Pecks Lake, and many more feed hydroelectric stations downstream. The great Gilboa Reservoir on the Schoharie supplies New York City with drinking water and the Blenheim-Gilboa Pumped Storage Project on the same river produces one million kilowatts twelve hours a day. Power is also produced at Lock 7, at Cohoes, and at many other places on the main river.

Many of the smaller falls, tucked away in shaded canyons and glens, bedecked with mosses and flowers, are of surpassing beauty. Have you seen the twin Plotterkill Falls in springtime or in winter? Have you seen Moccasin Flower Falls? Bouck Falls? Minekill Falls? To find these and scores more in the Mohawk watershed will take years of exploration.

Portions of twelve counties comprising 3,456 square miles make up the watershed. Albany, Schenectady, Saratoga, Montgomery, Fulton, Hamilton, Herkimer, Lewis, Oneida, Madison, Delaware, and Greene are within its boundaries. Substantial portions of the watershed forests in the mountainous regions are protected by Article XIV, Section 1, the "forever wild" covenant in the state constitution. This assures a continuously improved forest cover and more stable stream flow as forests mature, since the water-holding capacity of the soil increases steadily as leaves and needles fall, and trees and leaves and plants dissolve into duff or humus. Such protection also affords maximum protection from forest fires that could destroy this fragile, water-holding ecology.

Bison, caribou, and elk tramped trails to this valley from the West. A succession of Indian tribes followed these natural trailways centuries before modern peoples made highways of them. About A.D. 1400, the Iroquois occupied this great Mohawk River valley. Undoubtedly the richness of the terrain and its wonderful river resource helped to make them and their nation great.

The canoes plied the waters of most of the tributaries, which penetrated to wilderness heartlands where the moose, deer, bear, marten, and, most valuable of all, the beaver were plentiful. With the coming of the fur traders, the river became an avenue of trade. The records indicate that as many as eighty thousand beaver pelts a year got through to Albany; from which point, after taxes on them were paid, they were shipped to Europe for the hat-making industry.

One of the region's noted historians, George W. Featherston-haugh, clearly indicated the role of the river in early days. He wrote:

> From the close of the Revolution until the opening of the Erie Ca-nal in 1825, Schenectady was a lively river port, and boat building was one of the town's leading industries. Bateaux, Durham, and so-called Schenectady boats at first had a capacity of from one to two tons, and were propelled by oars, poles, and sails. Up the swift parts of the river, or riffs, they were helped by men on shore who dragged at ropes. In 1792 the Inland Lock and Navigation Com-pany, by building locks and canals at Little Falls, German Flats, and Rome, made it possible to employ boats of from ten to twenty tons capacity and even quite comfortable passenger packets with roofed and curtained cabins. Freight came over from Albany by wagon to the docks on the Binnekill, and to facilitate this traffic, stone tramways were built in the middle of the turnpike on the sand hills east of Schenectady.

It will thus be seen that the Erie Canal—greatest in the world of that day—came into being by an evolutionary process. From the earli-est days, the waters of the Mohawk, fed by great virgin forests sur-rounding the main valley, were vital to all that has happened in the val-ley since. The river actually gave its native occupants access by water to a very large portion of the colonies and to the unexplored West as far as the Mississippi. The early missionaries, the frontiersmen, the farmers, engineers, and scientists were to a large degree attracted here by the richness of this watershed.

The latest and most reliable information on hydroelectric dams on the rivers and tributary streams of the Mohawk puts that number at 147.

I will always remember that wonderful October afternoon when I sat on a cliff edge of the Helderberg Mountains with a friend, an inter-nationally recognized craftsman. Shadows were lengthening across the plain about a thousand feet below us, deepening the flaming colors of the foliage. Distant mountains surrounding the capital region were sof-tened by a misty haze. I told him about the Adirondacks and experi-ences in the wilderness I had known. He told me about the far regions of the world he had been to, of the great rivers and falls he has seen. He pointed northeasterly to the Mohawk Valley. "There," he said, "is the most beautiful waterscape in the whole world!"

3

The Moose River Wilderness

Trail to Moose River Plains. Conservation pioneers—John S. Apperson *(left)*, Allen Wilcox *(center)*, and Ed Richard *(right)*—and the beginning of a legal journey that took eleven years to complete.

N̲o issue in this century concerning the Adirondacks remotely compares with the eleven-year battle to preserve the South Branch of the Moose River from inundation by Higley Mountain and Panther Mountain dams.

Beginning in 1945 when bulldozers were ready to move in past Fawn Lake and down the Red River valley, conservationists waged war against the commercial interests all set to destroy one of the most beautiful of all Adirondack regions. They found that all the necessary papers had been signed, the conservation commissioner and the New York State Water Power and Control Commission had given the go-ahead, and once this action had been taken the project could not be legally halted. Higley Mountain dam was ready to be constructed.

So an attack was launched in the legislative and political arenas. Within two years, Governor Dewey reluctantly acceded to Speaker of the Assembly Heck and stopped the dam on political grounds. Then he immediately approved a larger reservoir downstream—Panther Mountain dam. Legislation was offered and rejected; legal injunctions were filed without success. But the battle raged on for three more years, and finally the New York State Legislature and the governor approved a bill banning all dams to regulate the flow of the Moose River.

This was not an entirely satisfactory answer to the aroused public. What about the fact that the statute could be rescinded at some later date? What about the thirty more reservoirs on the Water Power and Control Commission's maps already engineered? The answer was clear but seemingly not achievable: repeal the constitutional amendment of 1913 that authorized 3 percent of the New York State Forest Preserve to be inundated! Three more years of hard, unceasing work resulted in that repeal.

But then the roof fell in on the conservationists. The New York State Senate and Assembly passed an amendment permitting construction of Panther Mountain dam under terms of the repealed amendment. They did so twice, and it was due for the people's vote in referendum. Two more years of intense activity followed by the greatest coalition of conservationists ever to join in such a battle: the Adirondack Moose River Committee, the New York State Conservation Council, the Izaak

Walton League of America, the Association for the Protection of the Adirondacks, the Adirondack Mountain Club, the Forest Preserve Association of New York State, the Federated Garden Clubs joined with service clubs, bird clubs, trail conferences, churches, and labor unions. Backing these groups were an almost united media, especially when key statesmen and political organizations joined the fray. Tremendous support was also given by many national groups such as the Wilderness Society, the National Wildlife Federation, the Wildlife Management Institute, the American Nature Association, the National Parks Association, and many more. On election day, hundreds, if not thousands, of sportsmen passed out information at the polls, and a youthful group of rough-riders on horseback distributed brochures in the hills of the Mohawk Valley.

Never before had there been such an outpouring of a people determined that their hopes and dreams for posterity should not be denied them. Against this overwhelming sentiment were groups such as the Black River Regulating District Board and its commercial contacts, the Associated Industries of New York State, the New York State Conference of Mayors, and other commercial groups, as well as certain county legislatures of the region involved.

The vote for Panther Mountain dam in the referendum was 613,000; the vote against the dam was 1,622,000. The overwhelming vote had a profound impact on many other conservation issues related to the Adirondacks and Catskills. It is doubtful that many of the great achievements in the field of conservation throughout New York State could have been possible if there had not been this kind of battle and this kind of victory.

Despite the overwhelming vote, the proponents of Panther Mountain dam took the case to the United States Supreme Court. The Court refused to hear the case on the basis that the courts of New York had so clearly supported the opposition in the three supreme court actions, three appellate court actions, and four by the Court of Appeals.

One of the persistent arguments for the construction of Higley Mountain and Panther Mountain dams was that only a relatively small portion of the forest preserve would be taken and that much of the land was private and of little consequence to the people of New York State.

In July 1948, I attempted to provide an answer to this philosophy and wrote the following in an issue of the *Forest Preserve*:

> This is *Adirondack* land. It is within the great Adirondack Park. It is an irreplaceable portion of a magnificent wild region. Build your

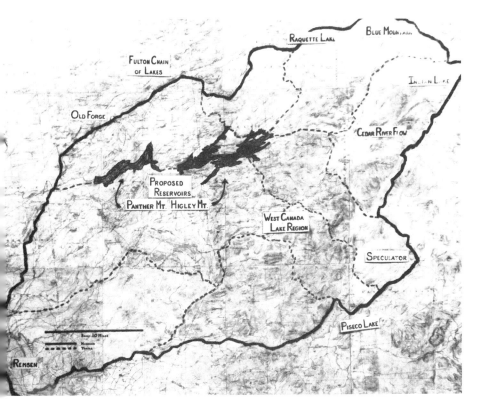

Map showing locations of Panther Mountain dam *(left)* and Higley Mountain dam *(right)* on the Moose River within the one-thousand-square-mile Moose River wild area.

regulating reservoirs, if you will, in areas where serious forest and wildlife values will not be destroyed. Leave this valley of the South Branch of the Moose River alone, that it may serve its highest use which is preservation in its natural state.

A citizen may not have title to his home, but he does have an undivided deed to this Adirondack land of solitude and peace and tranquillity. To him belong the sparkling lakes tucked away in the deep woods and the cold, pure rivers which thread like quicksilver through lush mountain valleys. His determination to preserve this personal treasure for posterity has been tempered by memories of flickering campfires, and strengthened by pack-laden tramps along wilderness trails and mountaintop views of his chosen land.

To him the South Branch of the Moose is a River of Opportunity for he has come to regard it as the front line of defense against the commercial invasion of *his* forest preserve.

. . . he is watching with a kind of breathless anxiety the fate of this valley. He feels that the issue concerns his basic rights as a citizen of New York State.

The Adirondack
THE MAKING OF A RELIEF MAP

The genesis of our relief map of the Adirondack Mountains was the realization, when we were faced with critical conservation issues, that our knowledge of the Adironack Park was very limited. Like several associates, I had been exploring these mountains for several decades, hunting, fishing, and backpacking into remote regions. These interests became secondary in 1931 when we began missions for John S. Apperson, a noted exponent of the "forever wild" covenant. He needed firsthand data and photographs of key regions to support his ongoing battles to preserve the region. We began pouring over maps and documents and learning the basics of motion-picture photography for creating films he believed were essential for public understanding of complicated issues, especially those related to the valuable watershed forests and the erosion of lake shores and islands.

At the time, the New York State Legislature had twice approved an amendment to the forest protective covenant that would have permitted any authority—state, county, or town—to construct closed cabins in the New York State Forest Preserve. Approval of this proposal by the people would have doomed the possibility of protected wilderness in the Adirondacks. Happily, the public reacted with statewide opposition, initiated by Apperson and his films, and soundly defeated the threat.

We had begun to have illusions that we knew the Adirondacks. Then one day I was sufficiently chastened by my lack of knowledge of many regions of the park that I decided to do something about it. It came about this way.

Reprinted from *Adirondack Life*, May 1986.

Relief map in Paul Schaefer's Adirondack Library. In 1945 George Marshall's question about the proposed dams on the Moose River triggered two significant actions: the first was the creation of a full-scale relief map of the Adirondacks, and the second was the historic battle to save the Moose River country from inundation. Photograph by Tom Carney.

As a member of the Adirondack Mountain Club, I found myself at the club's annual dinner in New York City in 1945. I had become a friend of Russell M. L. Carson, author of *Peaks and People of the Adirondacks*, and he had urged my attendance. It was probably he who arranged my dinner seat to be directly opposite that of George Marshall, renowned Forty-sixer, whom I had never met, although I had met his brother Bob on top of Mount Marcy a dozen years earlier. George began asking me questions.

"What do you know about proposed dams on the Moose River? Are there one or two? Will they flood out the virgin Beaver Lake and Indian River country? What will happen to the deer if their winter yarding ground on the plains is inundated?" Then he said, "Last week I saw in Washington a United States Army Engineer's map labeled *Panther Mountain Reservoir, South Branch of the Moose River*."

With that I frankly admitted that I knew nothing about the Moose River and nothing of the dams. I was embarrassed because I was one of those who professed to know something about the Adirondacks but actually was quite ignorant of vast regions of that ten-thousand square mile park. I promised George Marshall that I would immediately check out the river and be in touch with him.

On the way home from that meeting, the idea of a relief map came forcibly to me. I kept remembering the scores of United States Geological Survey maps, which we had been pouring over for years, and how unsatisfactory they generally were, especially when trying to follow rivers and mountains that coursed out of individual maps. At least, I thought, they ought to be all together, easily visible in their entire relationship to one another. And then—why not—an accurate relief map of the whole mountain system?

Several days later, I proposed the idea to the Albany chapter of the Adirondack Mountain Club of which I was a member and asked for volunteers. Fate, at this moment, was very kind. For immediately after my presentation, a tall gentleman stood up and said that since he had been in charge of relief-map making for the military invasion forces in the South Pacific, he might be able to help. He was Colonel William Hannah of the United States Army.

Several days later, he was in my library in Niskayuna explaining to a wide-eyed group of my mountain-climbing friends the techniques of relief-map making. We moved on it the very next day, getting maps and cardboard and glue and carbon paper. We were off on a project that was to take nine years effort by fifty individuals and thirteen thousand hours to complete. We found volunteers in a forest ranger, a con-

The Adirondack Room. Here is a place that for decades has symbolized battles for the integrity of the New York State Forest Preserve. Eight organizations were formed within its walls, including
two that represent more than a thousand clubs. Hundreds of meetings, many of these involving state agencies and legislative committees, were held here, where the Adirondack relief map and library
are also housed.

servation department biologist, a woman captain in the air force,
a national conservation leader, scientists from the General Electric
Company, a carpenter, a stonemason, my family of aspiring Forty-
sixers, and all manner of people. One person after another agreed to
trace one of the sixty United States Geological Survey topographical
maps. Week after week, month after month, year after year, it progressed. All volunteers. Donald Bordwell, a building trades craftsman,
painstakingly cut all of the elevation lines on all of the maps— he was
there on the first day of the map project and on its day of completion,

nine years later. The entire effort spawned an organization which was vital in ensuing battles—the Friends of the Forest Preserve.

Again fate presented me with a rearkable coincidence. Within ten day of meeting with George Marshall in New York, I met Edmund Richard of Fort Plain at one of Apperson's frequent meetings held to plan strategy. I asked him what he knew about the Moose River. Astonishingly, he had spent considerable time on the plains studying deer with the biologists of the New York State Conservation Department. He told me that Alan Wilcox, who owned the virgin Beaver Lake, was absolutely discouraged about the prospect of the devastation of that lake and all the surrounding country by the proposed Higley Mountain dam. The Black River Regulating District had had final orders signed and court actions completed to construct it. Bulldozers were ready to move in.

I was shocked, and Ed suggested that we at once contact Allen Wilcox on Fourth Lake and see if anything further could be done. Several days later we were there, and they arranged with the renowned bush pilot, Harold Scott of Inlet, to fly me over the region involved.

On a cold, clear September day, we had climbed in Scotty's open-cockpit amphibian and reached the height of about a mile. Then he leaned over and shouted at me above the roar of the motor, "The next time you look down you'll see it all."

And I did!

Forests unlimited, dotted with lakes sparkling in the sunshine. Rivers threading like quicksilver through the plains and into the evergreen woods westerly. The crowns of giant pines rising above the green canopy of woods. Trails twisting down along the Red River to the Moose and disappearing in wilderness. And in the distance, to all points of the compass, mountain on mountain fading into far horizons.

There, I thought, was the relief map!

And on that day the battle over that valley began again; nor was it to end until ten years later when both Higley Mt. dam, Panther Mt. dam, and a host of lesser dams had been relegated to the wastebasket by the most overwhelming outpouring of sentiment by the public, the press, and by various organizations in the history of the state!

At our first meeting, Colonel Hannah had suggested that we mount the map on a vertical twelve-foot-high wall of my library which has an open gable ceiling. Accordingly we built a plywood base twelve feet high and about ten feet wide, inclined inward about a foot. On this base, we assembled the quadrangles—sixty-two of them, averaging about twelve by seventeen inches and each encompassing about two hundred square miles of country. These maps would have the one-hundred-foot contours traced on cardboard, cut out and gradually assembled one upon the other until all the hills and mountaintops had been reached. Over this basic relief, spackling compound would be spread, carefully molding it to express the elevations on the maps. When dry, a form was made and plaster of paris poured to cover it. From that negative, after the cardboard model was removed, the final positive plaster was cast.

As the weeks and months and years went on, semifinished maps replaced the survey maps on the base. Mountain ranges and rivers were joined, and at long last the final relief was ready for painting.

Mountains, lakes, rivers, towns, and villages began showing up in the strangest places. We could hardly believe what the relief map was telling us. How the glaciers swept from northeast to southwest, where the eskers were, how the rivers snaked between the mountains, where the roads had to be built. Place a finger across that river and lo—look at that land that would be flooded! And look at the potential for wilderness over there. And all that flat, lake-spangled land—what a water wilderness that would make!

One day in the early 1950s, I had made a progress statement to the Association for the Protection of the Adirondacks in New York City. Harold Hochschild, a vice president, was there. He requested that his architects see the map and if they approved, it would be in his new museum at Blue Mountain Lake. Within a week, approval was given, and we were asked to make a second copy. Our total involvement with the Moose River dams battle made that impossible, but our molds were made available and the fine map at the museum was cast from them by a major map corporation.

A relief map such as ours is a project that will never be completely finished. We have to add more details as more is learned about the mountains. In 1921, Alfred Donaldson began his *History of the Adirondacks* by stating that the Adirondacks consisted "of about one hundred mountains from 1,200 to 5,000 feet in height." There are two thousand mountains! A decade ago we were telling unbelieving audiences that there were one thousand five hundred lakes in the Adirondack Park. There are about two thousand eight hundred! Just last winter, several hundred hours of painstaking work completed the last of the hundreds of streams shown on topographic maps. And also we added one lovely glacial lake we had found in the 1960s, one not shown on any map— state or national!

We will add other features as the uses of the Adirondacks continue to be refined. We added the Northway, which was only a dream at the time we began the map. Soon there will be an interpretive center, not far from the celebrated Adirondack Museum. Someday we might show all the state land as acquisitions continue. Could we do it in a paint visible only under certain lights? What about the gradual implementation of hydro units on the sites of the early water-powered mills? How can we bring out economic developments, hidden as they will be, within this vast area of mountains and forests? Can we plot the hopes and dreams for the Adirondacks as they might be at the second centennial?

It is hoped that this map, born of admitted lack of understanding of the park, can play an ever more important role in refining this unique and magnificent region.

Land of giant trees.

The Impending Tragedy of the
Moose River Region

The South Branch of the Moose River rises on Little Moose Mountain just west of the Cedar River Flow in the central Adirondacks. It flows westerly towards the Fulton Chain of Lakes country, bisecting for about thirty miles the most extensive primitive area in these mountains.

Here is a land roughly forty miles long by twenty-five miles wide, dotted with lakes and ponds and threaded with rivers and streams. It is heavily forested and without clearings, except for the unique natural Moose River Plains which are situated near the heart of this region.

It is a land of vast distances and solitude and yet despite its remoteness is surprisingly accessible. Good foot and saddle trails reach the interior, while amphibian planes make even the wildest pond accessible from Long Lake or the Fulton Chain of Lakes in a matter of minutes.

The mountains are not tall but present rounding contours which dip gracefully into myriad lakes and ponds of every description. Spruce and balsam dominate the long reaches of valley, with pine and hardwoods covering the ridges and hills.

It is this region along the South Branch of the Moose River that would be inundated by construction of the proposed Higley Mountain and Panther Mountain reservoirs.

An official report of the New York State Water Power and Control Commission reads in part:

> Pending before Congress is a war department report on a study of the Black and Moose Rivers. It recommends construction

Friends of the Forest Preserve brochure, September 1945.

of a multipurpose reservoir at Panther Mountain on the Moose River. This reservoir, estimated to cost $3,800,000, would be located about eight miles east of McKeever in Herkimer County.

Stream flow regulation, with a view towards development of hydroelectric power, is the primary purpose of the proposed reservoir. Flood control is a secondary consideration. Because of the nature of the proposed project, its prosecution and the requisite of local cooperation is a matter of direct concern, not to the Flood Control Commission, but to the Black River Regulating District Board.

As recommended, Panther Mountain reservoir will have a storage capacity of 278,000 acre feet, of which only 16 percent will be reserved solely for flood control utilization. The Black River Regulating District Board has indicated willingness to participate in the project.

Higley Mountain reservoir would be located about six miles upstream, or about fourteen miles east of McKeever. Its purpose is primarily stream flow regulation.

This latter reservoir would be built largely on forest preserve land and would put the Moose River Plains under more than forty feet of water. Helldiver Pond, Icehouse Pond, Beaver Lake, and the Lost Ponds would be inundated, as would the best sections of the Red and Indian rivers, and the Sumner, the Otter, and other streams.

The Moose River Plains is known to be the largest winter yarding grounds for deer in the Adirondacks. It is estimated that more than one thousand deer seek the food and shelter of this region in the winter. For many years the conservation department has conducted surveys of deer in this region. The outline of the proposed reservoirs' water level is substantially the winter shelter area of these great deer herds.

Winter shelter and winter food are the limiting features as regards the number of deer in the Adirondacks. It follows, therefore, that this largest of all deer herds in the Adirondacks will in all probability be exterminated, and the region for miles around will lose the source of its extraordinary deer population.

The character of the region, plus the distances involved in traversing it, make this region a sanctuary and source of many other animals including the bear, the otter, the fisher and other less common animals. Bird life is abundant, with the ruffed grouse having ideal conditions of habitat.

Fishermen come hundreds of miles to enjoy the superb trout

waters of the region. Not only will the rivers and ponds lose their trout with the creation of the reservoirs, but innumerable tributary streams will be destroyed for this fish. It is doubtful whether pike and similar fish could be kept out of the reservoirs. Their presence would finish the trout in this area.

The Moose River region is one of the finest remnants of natural woodland left in eastern America. The region is large enough, remote enough, and primitive enough to be one of the outstanding scenic attractions in all America. It is a land that attracts naturalist and hiker, as well as hunter and fisherman. It has values that are intangible and beyond adequate description. It is an attraction that beckons tourists from far places so that they might see and feel and understand the primeval beauty of the Adirondacks.

The construction of Panther Mountain and Higley Mountain reservoirs is naturally supposed to be of economic value to the state or region, directly or indirectly. But what are the economic losses caused by such reservoirs?

Of great importance to the region and the state is the abundance of fish and game. This factor alone is of great significance in the attraction of tourists who delight in a vacationland in which the deer and other animals are plentiful. This is a value that constantly increases down through the years and represents an enormous economic value to the state and the community. To replace a land of lakes and forests and rivers with millponds surely is of no economic advantage to these communities, which are already blessed with an abundance of water and power.

In the case of the Higley Mountain reservoir, public hearings have already been held, certiorari actions dismissed, and the Black River Regulating District Board is ready to go ahead with the project. The public hearings on the Panther Mountain project are expected to be held shortly.

It may thus be seen by this brief summary of the situation that with the completion of these proposed reservoirs, the Adirondacks will lose, in a single, devastating stroke, its largest deer-wintering grounds, the heart of its most extensive wild area, substantial virgin forests, and probably the best hunting and fishing area in these mountains.

An imposing number of statewide organizations have already gone on record against one or both of these proposed reservoirs and include such organizations as the Adirondack Mountain Club, the Izaak Walton League, and others. To date, however, no united action by these or other groups has occurred.

Immediate action by the leaders of existing organizations to form a statewide committee, which could spotlight the issues involved, may be the only action that can save the Moose River region from destruction.

Beyond Moose River Plains

Twilight was slowly setting over the Moose River Plains when we reached the log bridge which spans the South Branch of the Moose River just above the still water. This was the second day; behind us lay a long, winding snowshoe trail beginning at Sumner Lake just below Raquette, down the Sumner stream to the Lost Ponds, up through a grand forest to the historic Moose River trail, then the long, steady downgrade to the plains. The snow was deep and fluffy here and a twenty-below-zero wind from the west made trail-breaking an effort.

Travel is slow when cameramen dominate the party and the land is so full of interest and beauty. And when the four who tramp the trail are members of the Adirondack Moose River Committee one can understand the countless stops, here for a color shot, there a black and white, here a towering pine, there two deer bounding across the trail.

The Moose River was ice-locked. Its south bank was heavily forested with spruce; the north bounded the semiopen plains and had a scattering of evergreens and much brush which indicated heavy browsing by the deer herds that winter in the region. The Beaver Lake trail climbed the hill in front of us and the day being almost over, we adjusted our packs and headed into the land beyond the plains.

In the half-light of evening, we passed the largest trees we had yet seen. Here and there along the trail a giant pine nearly five feet in diameter rose into the sky, its storm-battered crown in magnificent silhouette against the sky. I was glad someone else chose to break trail most of this part of the trip, for it was easy to keep my bearpaws in broken trail while my eyes took in the full beauty of these forest giants. Night had

Reprinted from the *Adirondac*, March–April 1946, by permission of the Adirondack Mountain Club.

John Apperson in virgin forest at Indian River. A friend said during the battle against Higley Mountain dam, "It is the most wonderful country I ever want to see. In all things it is unsurpassed." John Apperson and I snowshoed through these virgin pines along the Indian River in February 1946. We were both almost speechless at the beauty that we saw.

overtaken us by the time we reached the crest of the ridge and began dropping into the basin gemmed by Beaver Lake.

We shall not soon forget that night at the cabin! It was bitter cold outside, but thirty-degrees-below-zero temperatures, which had prevailed for several days previously, had permeated the cabin which was well insulated with snow, and required that we open the door and let some of the warm zero air inside. Fortunately we had come with extra supplies and someone had slipped in a half-pint of Old Crow. I had developed hypothermia and was thankful for extra sleeping bags and some of the whiskey. Outside the overcast sky began to break up as the wind veered and the temperature dropped again. The last thing I remembered before dropping off to sleep was someone quoting Robert Service:

> The winter! The brightness that blinds you,
> The white land locked tight as a drum,
> The cold fear that follows and finds you,
> The silence that bludgeons you dumb,
> The snows that are older than history,
> The woods where the weird shadows slant,
> The stillness, the moonlight, the mystery,
> I bade them good-by—I can't.

The morning was brilliant with occasional snow puffs sweeping across the ice-crusted surface of Beaver Lake. It is doubtful if anywhere there can be a shoreline more beautiful than Beaver's with its immense pines and spruces rising clifflike from the water's edge. It is a mellow-brown page from Charles Fenno Hoffman's *Wild Scenes in the Forest* of a century ago!

This day will be with me always.

Snowshoeing across Beaver Lake we reached its southwest shore and hiked through the forest preserve down along Beaver River to the Indian River. I recalled the words expressed by a fellow conservationist as he embarked with us on this battle for the Moose River country: "It is the most magnificent country I ever want to see. In all things it is unsurpassed."

The Indian River flows northerly from a still water into the Moose. The lower portion is rapid as it twists along a pine-studded bluff to the east. This indeed is a remnant of the best there ever was in the Adirondacks!

Spruce and balsam intermingled with pine, and an occasional hardwood found survival possible. Under much of the area of these trees, we found considerable deer food in the form of buck brush and maple, which the deer were browsing extensively.

Every now and again, we saw a deer or two bounding easily away through the woods.

Wherever one turned, one saw a picture. We were glad we loaded down with film packs, for the day was one of sunlight and shadow, and constantly changing from one to the other in split seconds.

It was difficult to leave the Indian River. We did so with regret and the intention to come back as soon as opportunity permitted.

Virgin forest at Beaver Lake. All of this land would have been flooded by Higley Mountain dam.

The afternoon sunset across the lake was mixed with heavy storm clouds from the west. The thermometer was dropping slightly again, and this assured a good trip out the next several days.

What experience equals a long winter's evening with congenial companions in such a cabin retreat? Warm and dry, we lingered long over a meal which beggars description and ended with fresh, red apples from a nearby cache. It was an evening of tall tales, made fruitful by patching a snowshoe harness, waterproofing boots and the many other little things that make up life in the woods. Outside a giant pine cracked spasmodically, and the moon rode high in a sky flecked with clouds riding a fast wind.

Dawn on the trail is fascinating. Our return was blessed with fine camera weather, and the big trees really took a beating. We divided on the ridge above the Moose River, agreeing to join later at the log bridge. This was accomplished about fifty photographs later. We swapped ex-

The guide rose at dawn, renewed the fire, and soon had a hearty breakfast on the table. The thermometer registered minus forty degrees. I decided to snowshoe to the plains and to Icehouse Pond. The day was brilliantly clear. A fox ran across the lake ahead of me, and several deer were crossing at its far end.

periences and learned that a deer had graciously walked into a picture on the still water.

Details of the plains were carefully noted on the way out. To say the least, they are fascinating. The surrounding forest has, in the last half century or so, made considerable inroads upon this once open grassland. In places trees bisect the plains completely. Other areas, some twenty to forty feet below the general level of the plains, are thickly covered with evergreens, affording the most perfect protection for deer imaginable. Deer tracks were more abundant than I had ever seen, and at this time they were feeding to a considerable extent on the grass roots on the plains. New browsing on the many different kinds of brush was continually in evidence.

A highlight of the trip for me was a lone trip to Icehouse Pond, which lies between the Great Plains and the Little Plains. I had seen the pond from the air several times, and it was a gem. It upheld expectations as I walked over its frozen surface. Two deer, a bobcat, and a fox preceded me by a few minutes. The pond lays perhaps ten feet below the general level of the Little Plains and, though small, is exquisite in detail. To the east is a pine ridge, which seemed to be full of deer. Five of them jumped up close by, bounded a few paces, and looked back at me. Others were heard leaving the vicinity.

The following noon we saw the open expanse of Sumner Lake and the end of a near forty-mile tramp was in sight.

We all renewed our determination that this valley of the Moose River must always remain the heritage of posterity.

Land of the Deer

The Moose River region in New York State comprises about a thousand square miles of unbroken woodland in the southwestern part of the Adirondack Park. Near the heart of this rich, lush land are the famous Moose River Plains, a wild, apparently natural meadow of about seven hundred acres. This is, as it has been for many centuries, the land of the white-tailed deer. "Here several thousand deer winter every year in an area some ten miles long by from one half to two miles wide. This is not a yard in the popular sense, but a yarding ground where the deer from much of the surrounding territory congregate during the winter and over which they range in small groups of from five or six to ten or twelve each." The New York State Conservation Department, authority for the above statement, has used this Moose River area for about fifteen years as a place in which to study the deer, because it is the best and most extensive deer habitat in the state.

The naturalist could hardly wish for a land more abundant in wildlife. If he understands the region, he can watch scores of deer feeding together on lily pads on one of the numerous little lakes, or see them swimming together when their horns are in the velvet, or see them watching him from the depths of the forest. In winter he will find that the deer have indeed taken over the land, for it is possible to see hundreds of them in the course of several days during this season, and if one will but live with them a while at this time, they may be approached closely.

Here also may be found the less common animals such as the otter, the fisher and the marten as well as the bear and the bay lynx.

The Adirondacks truly is the "Land of the Deer."

Snowshoe rabbits, grouse and many smaller species round out what probably represents as near a primitive balance of wildlife as can be found anywhere in eastern North America.

An outstanding feature of the area is the virgin white pine. The pines tower above the spruce and hemlock and attain a trunk diameter of five feet at four feet above the ground. While these pine forests are not extensive in the sense that they consist of vast numbers of such trees, it is true that during the course of a recent forty-mile snowshoe trip through this region we were seldom if ever out of sight of these magnificent trees.

The heart of this land will soon be flooded out if the plans of the Black River Regulating District Board are carried out and Higley and

Panther Mountain reservoirs are created on the South Branch of the Moose River.

Must we virtually lose our choicest possessions before we fully realize their value?

During the darkest days of the war in 1942, public hearings were held in a small upstate town and a conservation commissioner finally approved the plans for Higley Mountain reservoir. Currently the federal government is contemplating aid for the construction of Panther Mountain reservoir which has so recently figured in a trespass claim by the state against the Black River Board for unlawfully cutting several thousand trees on forest preserve land. Hydroelectric power, rather than flood control, is the primary purpose of both contemplated reservoirs.

As recently as September 1945, no conservation, sportsmen's or civic club was fighting the proposals, simply because the proposals were not known to them. As a result of the Adirondack Mountain Club's Conservation Forum held in Albany last October, the Adirondack Moose River Committee was formed. From its inception it has enjoyed the almost united support of outdoor-minded New Yorkers, including sportsmen's and conservation associations from one end of the state to the other. It recognized from the first that the issue was all but lost and that it had little legal recourse; it staked its position on the fact that, if the people did not want the Moose River valley destroyed, the force of public opinion could accomplish what would be impossible by any other means.

A panel of speakers was formed to explain the issue and to describe an outstanding Kodachrome moving picture and slides of the region which were taken by members of the committee. Several duplicates were made, and the story is being made clear all across the state. The press and the radio are becoming increasingly outspoken as the opposition has been consolidating its gains.

As a result of this combined action by many groups, a bill was introduced in the New York State Legislature on February 21, 1946, by Leo A. Lawrence, chairman of the Assembly Conservation Committee. It amends Section 459 of the Conservation Law and reads as follows: "Construction of new or additional regulating reservoirs is prohibited in the Adirondack Park. Notwithstanding any inconsistent provision of this chapter or of any other law, no reservoirs for the regulation of the flow of streams hereafter shall be constructed by any board within the boundaries of the Adirondack Park."

On February 27, 1946, a public hearing was held on this bill in the state capitol. Five individuals representing two regulating boards

U.S. Army Corps of Engineers' survey markings, Higley Mountain. Everything below this topographical mark and everything above it for thirty-five feet would have been inundated by the waters of the proposed Higley Mountain dam. This would have destroyed three lakes and the winter yarding grounds for more than a thousand deer.

and one club appeared against the proposal with more than thirty individuals representing more than five hundred clubs appearing in favor of the bill. A strong fight for passage is now being made.

There is a lesson to be learned in a brief study of the basic principles involved in this issue. Thirty-one years ago the people of New York State approved an amendment to that part of their constitution requiring that "the lands of the state, constituting the forest preserve . . . shall be forever kept as wild forest lands." The amendment permitted the use of up to 3 percent of such forest preserve lands for stream flow regulation, for municipal water supply and for the canals of the state. It was determined then that hydroelectric power could be but an incidental purpose of such reservoirs, but this meaning has been misconstrued to the point where the regulating districts openly state that power is a primary purpose of such stream flow regulation.

The big point, however, is the fact that while three percent of several million acres seems a very small area indeed, it is now realized that this lowland acreage is by far the most valuable land of the Adirondack Park. This is the "green land"; the sheltered land, the winter home and refuge of the deer and other animals. When the deep snows and the frigid Arctic winds of winter sweep over northern New York, it is to these lands that wildlife retreats, life being impossible without the food and shelter of these lowlands. Since both winter shelter and winter food are the limiting features as regards the abundance of such wildlife, it follows that the future of Adirondack fauna rests upon the maintenance of this cover in the Adirondacks. To flood out the sheltered evergreen basins throughout these mountains is to automatically eliminate the home and cradle of such wildlife, as well as the wild forest character of the forest preserve, replacing all this with dams and fluctuating water levels, eroding shorelines, and mud flats.

The scientific findings of the State of Wisconsin's Conservation Department as set forth in their publication No. 321 says: "State after state reports instances of deer refusing to leave (or even be driven from) a depleted winter range. Paraphrased in human terms, 'deer would rather starve than move.'"

With respect to the proposed Moose River reservoirs, the high-flow line of the reservoirs, set at 1,716 feet above sea level for Panther Mountain and 1,892 feet above sea level for Higley, represents very nearly the entire existing winter-feeding range for the deer in this valley. Above these elevations, there is little evergreen cover; the predominating trees being mixed hardwoods that give little or no protection from wintry blasts sweeping in from Lake Ontario and Canada. Thus we can understand why the Moose River deer herds—the largest in the East—would be exterminated if the reservoirs are built.

Other losses would be incurred along with the extermination of the deer. In a single stroke the Adirondacks would lose its best wildlife habitat, its unsurpassed trout waters, its most extensive primitive recreation land and some of the finest examples of virgin forest in the East. From the viewpoint of destruction of the wilderness character of the region, the proposed reservoirs would do a thorough job.

Originally thought to be the beaver hunting country of the Iroquois, it was here that the first hunters and trappers carried on their trade at about the time of the Revolution. Until less than a century ago, it was little known and seldom visited by any but hunters. With the advent of lumbering, parts of the region felt the axe, but a large part of it has belonged to the state for many years, or to such groups as the Adirondack League Club which did much to prevent despoilment of the region. Today the entire Moose River area, with the exception of the plains, remains heavily forested, with little evidence of erosion or burning, as contrasted with some other parts of the park which have been seriously devastated. The surrounding highways are for the most part lined with fine forest growth, and billboards and other obnoxious evidences of human activity are conspicuously absent.

Beyond the water limits of the reservoirs are many thousands of acres of state land, replete with lakes and ponds and containing innumerable trout waters. The miles of reservoir reaching up into this largest remnant of unbroken wilderness in the state would destroy with finality the existing solitude of the region. It takes little foresight to realize that the motorboat and amphibian plane would make the existing wild places quickly and easily accessible, and that the construction roads, planned around the reservoir shoreline, would hasten the end of this important and rare attraction.

The people of New York and the nation are making an unprecedented plea for the preservation of this region. It is logical to believe that in the current legislative effort to remove the danger inherent to all Adirondack lowlands, the people will make an all-out fight to successfully conclude the issue. And it is reasonable to believe that the people will urge the state to acquire more of this type of land for the increasing recreational needs of the people and for the protection of the natural forest regulators of stream flow.

If the principles involved in this issue are understood by a sufficient number of people, the values of an abundant wildlife, of forest, river and glacial lake will be enjoyed by succeeding generations for whom we hold this magnificent heritage in trust.

Victory in Defeat

The clock above the main entrance to the assembly chambers in the New York State Capitol indicated the time as 3:37 P.M. It was March 13, 1947. In the gallery above the one hundred and fifty elected representatives of the people, we had watched the hands tell the hours away, as legislators passed bills with clocklike precision. It had been a long vigil in which hope, suspense, and frustration followed each other predictably.

At last our time had come and the clerk was reading our bill: "Assembly print #1076, Introductory #1057 by Mr. Leo Lawrence. An act to amend the Conservation Law, in relation to prohibiting the construction of new or additional reservoirs on the South Branch of the Moose River by any river regulating district board."

The tenseness of the moment was broken by the speaker who introduced Assemblyman Leo P. Noonan. With dramatic gestures and an equally dramatic voice, Mr. Noonan introduced Mr. Lawrence of Herkimer County and his opponent, Mr. Demo of Lewis County, as a referee would introduce boxers in a championship contest. "The Queensbury rules and all other rules are waived," he said.

Assemblyman Lawrence quickly dispelled the comedy by announcing that "all rules of the game will be strictly observed." He then began his well-prepared speech in behalf of the preservation of the South Branch of the Moose River. He traced carefully the history of the forest preserve from its beginning in 1885 through three constitutional conventions to the present day. He brought out the administrative scandals that led to writing the protection of the public lands in the Adirondacks and Catskills into the state constitution where such resources could not be legislated away without the consent of the people. When he quoted

Reprinted from the *Cloudsplitter*, May–June 1947, by permission of The Cloudsplitter, Albany Chapter, ADK.

Indian River still water. Like a thread of quicksilver the river
pierced into a canyon of forest, until a wall of giant pine abruptly
ended the view, their storm-bent crowns lofty above the lesser
spruce and balsam. . . . It was an adventure into the dim and distant past, a glimpse of America before the advent of man with his
instruments of destruction and his carelessness with the treasures of
the good earth.

Article XIV, Section 1, of the New York State Constitution, which declares that "the lands of the state . . . shall be forever kept as wild forest lands," his voice was clear and strong and seemed to fill the chamber.

Mr. Lawrence reviewed the repeated attempts by commercial interests to remove or nullify the provision a convention had unanimously adopted a half century before. He brought out the fact that the people had consistently upheld this provision by their votes in referendums, and that during the current session they had demanded again that the proposed recreation and mining amendments be killed, as they were. He traced the history of the Black River Regulating District Board and stated that it was a history of exploitation and of failure to carry out the intent of the constitutional provision governing the use of the forest preserve. "They seek to ravage and invade our forest preserve, the land owned by the people, the common people, and contrary to the statutory law, they still want to reassert themselves and take this power." His voice was full of sincerity and conviction. One could not escape the feeling that this was, for better or worse, a historic moment in the history of the New York State Legislature.

Rebuttal of Mr. Lawrence came from Assemblyman D. Cady Herrick of Albany, who had previously indicated his approval of the Lawrence bill but now led the unprecedented Democratic vote against the measure. As Mr. Herrick spoke, we wondered what so staunch a friend of the forest preserve as the late Governor Alfred E. Smith would have said and done if he had seen members of his party being led into approval of exploitation of land he had fought so many years to preserve!

Assemblyman Benjamin H. Demo next took the floor. His plea was for such use of the forest preserve as would not interfere with the continued industrial expansion of the Black River valley.

In his rebuttal, Mr. Lawrence again lashed at the power interests and their repeated attempts to exploit the public lands when other great water resources, as the Saint Lawrence and other reservoir sites outside the Adirondack Park, were being neglected.

"The clerk will call the roll."

This was it! In a low monotone the clerk began. I was conscious at once of negative votes being cast but remembered no names except those in the affirmative.

"Mr. Bacon, Mr. Baczkowski, Mrs. Banks, Mr. Barrett, Mr. Bennett, Mr. Bennison, Mr. Bentley, Mr. Black, Mr. Cady, Mr. Brook, Mr. Combs, Mr. Coville, Mr. Creal, Mr. Crews, Mr. Cusick, Mr. Dannebrock, Mr. De Pasquale . . ."

As the affirmative and negative votes were recorded on the clerk's list just below me, my mind went back across the long, exciting journey which began twenty-one months before, when from a plane I had a first glimpse of the magnificent Moose River region. That day as we followed the thin ribbon of blue called the South Branch of the Moose, the land had sent up a call to me which I knew would soon have to be answered. And sure enough, a short time later we were packing on snowshoes into the most remote portions of that region and seeing, with unbelieving eyes, the glory of this wilderness.

"Mr. De Salvio, Mr. Doige, Mr. Douglas, Mr. Drohan, Mr. Drumm, Mr. Finch, Mr. Fitzpatrick, Mr. Fogarty, Mr. Galloway, Mr. Goldwater, Mrs. Gordon, Mr. Graber, Mr. Griffith, Mr. Gugino, Mrs. Hanniford, Mr. Hatfield . . ."

"The Moose River plains are a barren, desolate wasteland." Who, upon even the most casual exploration of the plains, could think so? Yet Black River Regulating District Board has referred to them as such in its statements to the press. Who could write that except one who has never seen the unique beauty of the plains, or one who, in the process of figuring stored horsepower, has lost forever the ability to evaluate properly the esthetic as opposed to the economic uses of such land?

For one who looks across the long reaches of the plains to the graceful shoulders of Wakely Mountain ten miles away, there will always remain a sense of vastness and wildness. And for one who explores the plains with its glacial lakes, its profusion of wildlife, and its ragged, wind-torn forests, there will always remain a memory of haunting beauty.

"Mr. Hill (T.), Mr. Hollinger, Mr. Johnson, Mr. Kaplan, Mr. Kellam, Mr. Knauf, Mr. Lashin, Mr. Lawrence (C.), Mr. Lawrence (L. A.), Mr. Lupton, Mr. Lyons, Mr. Marble, Mr. McCullough, Mr. McGivern, Mr. McGowan, Mr. Morgan . . ."

There was that day last September when we camped on Beaver Lake and watched the deer cavorting along the shores. A great blue heron stood stiff-legged in the shallow water, while deer walked within a few feet of it without disturbing it. There were two small fawns which played like children in the water, chasing each other for an hour up and down the beach and then losing themselves quickly in the green forest which rose like a curtain backdrop more than a hundred feet above the water. Only the day before, the guide had watched a lynx noiselessly walk down the shore toward the beach.

"Mr. Noonan, Mr. Ostrander, Mr. Parsons, Mr. Peck, Mr. Rabin, Mr. Radigan, Mr. Reoux, Mr. Riley, Mr. Roman, Mr. Rulison, Mr. Schneider, Mr. Schulman . . . "

"The trees are small in size and poor in form, spruce and balsam scrubby and excessively limby." How could the Black River Regulating District Board so describe the forests of the Higley Mountain basin? We had walked through heavy forests from the plains to Beaver Lake and thence to the Indian River. Occasionally a giant pine more than four feet in diameter and a hundred fifty feet high was passed along the trail. At length we reached a small island in the Indian, there where the riffles and the still water begins.

I think I shall never see a lovelier sight than lay before me that day! Like a thread of quicksilver the river pierced into a canyon of forest, until a wall of giant pines abruptly ended the view, their storm-bent crowns lofty above the lesser spruce and balsam. Grasses and ferns and flowers of the wilderness grew waist-deep on the banks which flanked the river, their varied hues reflecting brightly in the quiet waters. A well-worn deer trail skirted the stream and disappeared in the shadows. It was an adventure into the dim and distant past, a glimpse of America before the advent of man with his instruments of destruction and his carelessness with the treasures of the good earth.

"Mr. Shaw, Mr. Sirignano, Mr. Stuart, Mr. Sullivan, Mrs. Ten Eyck, Mr. Thompson, Mr. Tifft, Mr. Van Duzer, Mr. Volker, Mr. Walmsley, Mr. Ward, Mr. Younglove . . . "

There was a murmur of voices as the clerk called for sixteen absentees, of whom six had pledged us their vote. None answered.

"Affirmative 71 votes, negative 63 votes. The bill is defeated." The party record was: Affirmative—Republicans 60, Democrats 10, American Labor 1; Negative—Republicans 35, Democrats 28. Votes needed to carry a majority in the Assembly, 76.

It seemed impossible, yet it was true. Twenty-one months of ceaseless effort by the greatest number of clubs battling for the forest preserve in the history of the state. Thousands of citizens requesting, pleading and demanding that this irreplaceable land be preserved. Debates with our adversaries in their home territory with virtually unanimous decisions in our favor. The conservation commissioner fighting hard and consistently for the bill. The *New York Times,* the *Daily Mirror,* the *Buffalo Evening News,* the *Schenectady Gazette,* and dozens of other leading newspapers and magazines strongly editorializing for preservation of this land. The largest public hearing in the capitol in years almost unanimously fighting for the bill.

Attorneys for the Adirondack Moose River Committee and the Friends of the Forest Preserve began their papers of injunction as a last resort. Then came the statement from Speaker Oswald D. Heck's office:

The last thing the State of New York wants to do or should do is to spoil any part of its great forest preserve for purely commercial or trivial purposes. In particular we do not want our forest land despoiled unnecessarily for the purpose of creating water power . . . It is important that we get to the bottom of this whole problem, probe every angle of it, remote and apparent . . . The Governor has advised me that he intends to direct by an appropriate agency a thorough study of all of the ramifications of the flood control and water power program and its effect upon the forest preserve during the coming months. Pending completion of this study, the state will oppose any attempt to construct a dam in that area.

Who could with certainty account for such an unprecedented move? One thing is evident. Without the overwhelming sentiment of the people, expressed in every conceivable form and manner—the press, the radio, letters and wires by the mountain clubs, the sportsmen, the civic associations—it is a certainty that such action would not have been taken.

Thus the Moose River fight is not yet lost, nor is it won, for a long, difficult and complicated job looms ahead. Perhaps it will now be possible to lay down the basic principles involving such proposed flooding of the forest preserve. Perhaps we shall have the opportunity to bring out the tremendous economic value of resource preservation as against resource utilization in the Adirondack Park.

Who knows but that the Moose River battle may be the Valley Forge in which the hearts of the out-of-doors people were tried and found to be of a temper against which apparently overwhelming odds cannot prevail?

Against the Dam

For more than three years, a violent conflict has raged over the question of whether or not the natural features of the valley of the South Branch of the Moose River in the Adirondack Park shall be erased in favor of the proposed Higley and Panther mountain reservoirs.

Although the plans calling for the construction of these reservoirs had been offered in one form or another for nearly thirty years, it was not until 1945 that the issue was drawn by conservationists. Then, for the first time, they realized the magnitude of the problem they faced. It was this: should the people of New York State acquiesce in the proposal that the beautiful and game-abundant lowlands in the Adirondack mountains be permanently destroyed by the construction of thirty or more reservoirs, the water levels of which, by the very nature of the projects, would fluctuate so vastly that the wild forest character of the entire state park would be substantially destroyed?

In considering the problem, the overall effect of the master plans of the river-regulating districts was looked into. These plans called for the eventual construction of scores of reservoirs fairly evenly distributed throughout the Adirondack Park. The list of reservoir sites in addition to the Higley and Panther mountain areas includes Cedar River Flow, Piseco Lake, Lake Pleasant, the Essex Chain of Lakes, Goodnow Flow, Thirteenth Lake, Elm Lake, the Kunjamuk River, Schroon Lake, the Upper Hudson, Boreas Ponds, Indian Lake, and others. For some reason, it appears that this picture had never before been presented to the people of the state, who had at great expense and over a period of more than sixty years, gradually enlarged and perfected a forest preserve in the Adirondacks consisting of more than two million acres. It was gen-

Reprinted from the *Empire Statesman*, 1949.

Virgin forest in the Moose River country. Every so often along the trail, we came upon white pines larger in diameter and taller than we had ever seen before. They were truly magnificent.

erally understood by them that this land was, by the clear wording of a constitutional safeguard supposedly covering this land, to be forever kept inviolate from commercial use.

The catch was a little-understood amendment passed by the legislature in 1913 and approved by the people in 1915. It permitted the legislature by general laws to provide for reservoirs flooding not more than 3 percent of the total area of the forest preserve.

This seemed most reasonable at the time, for no conservationist was then, nor is now, opposed to genuine flood control projects. The Sacandaga Reservoir is an example of this type of river control, which has eliminated flood damage at Albany and Troy.

The Adirondack Moose River Committee was organized in Albany in 1945. It was a temporary, emergency coalition of conservation and sportsmen's organizations designed to halt if possible the immediate threats—the proposed Panther and Higley Mountain reservoirs.

The Higley Mountain area, a land of unsurpassed natural beauty, and largely state land, was the immediate focus of the effort to block unlawful usurpation of the public lands for power purposes. In this area are to be found the largest concentration of the white-tailed deer in the East, excellent brook trout fishing, and remnants of the magnificent virgin forest, which once covered New York State.

The effort was finally successful after several legislative failures. The Black River Regulating District Board yielded to the public pressure and administration policy by officially abandoning the proposal on May 8, 1948. But they did so only with the definite idea in mind that they would build the Panther dam some fourteen miles downstream on the same river.

Again the Adirondack Moose River Committee with its more than one thousand member organizations moved in on the proposal. Again it received virtually unanimous support from the press of the state and from many leading statesmen. The committee began an attack on three major fronts: the first an educational campaign to arouse public support, the second a carefully planned legal challenge of the constitutionality of the Panther dam, and the third a remedial action by the legislature.

The campaign against Panther dam has uncovered a most remarkable fact—a situation which the public, and even the legal profession, had no way of realizing until just a few months ago. This is the surprising fact that the law which set up the Black River Regulating Board is so carefully and shrewdly worded that the people of the State of New York are actually powerless to influence the board without, at great expense, going to court after the order for construction has been issued. For the New York State Water Power and Control Commission, which has always been assumed to have veto power over the Black River Board, has now claimed that it can, by law, only "accept or modify," any dam presented by the board for its consideration. The Water Power Commission has no legal power to represent the public interest but is concerned primarily with engineering problems.

To make matters even worse, anyone choosing to go to court to reverse an arbitrary decision of the Black River Board must put up a bond; and if the complainants lose their appeal, the Black River Board can make them pay for any costs accrued as a result of the court action. As it now stands, the board decides the time has come to build a dam; it submits plans to a state board which cannot reject them; holds a public hearing; then itself decides, with no interference from anyone, whether to pay any attention to the hearings it has held. Incidentally these hearings are held under conditions most unfair to objectors. Not only do they have no power of subpoena (which would have allowed objectors to produce all the witnesses against Panther dam they wanted), but the board acts as a prosecutor, judge, jury, and executioner. This is the reason why, after seven days of hearings in which dozens of witnesses appeared to testify against Panther dam, and very few for it, the board could and did say, "We intend to build Panther dam."

In the last session of the legislature, there was much agitation for revision of the conservation laws. For the 1949 session, there has already been a promise by several outstanding legislative leaders that the effort will be made to pass corrective legislation.

In a letter to the Schenectady County Conservation Council, Oswald D. Heck, Speaker of the Assembly said: "I am thoroughly in accord with your specific proposals of a referendum in which the people would have the opportunity to decide what is best for the preserve. Such a plan has great merit and should foredoom any objectionable construction within the forest preserve."

Moreover, Walter W. Stokes, head of the Conservation Committee of the Senate, has spoken out: "I have received so many personal letters and petitions in opposition to the building of the so-called Panther dam, that it has been utterly impossible for me to answer all of them. Therefore, I wish to say to my constituents and to the sportsmen of the State of New York generally, that I am unalterably opposed to building Panther or any other dam in the Adirondack Forest Preserve."

Senator Stokes further declared: "The building of any dam in the

Adirondack Forest Preserve for power purposes is, in my opinion, unconstitutional."

Leo A. Lawrence, Chairman of the Assembly Conservation Committee, is equally forthright in his opposition to flooding the Adirondacks. He has recently written: "You can certainly rest assured that I still vigorously oppose the invasion of the property of the commonwealth, and the destruction thereof by those desiring to enhance private interests. I shall certainly be happy to support the proposed amendment to Article XIV, Section 2, of the Constitution [eliminating stream flow regulation]."

In the meantime, the deadline for a petition for a writ of certiorari required that the legal action phase of the Panther dam case should get under way. This petition was presented to the Supreme Court on December 9, 1948, in Syracuse, signed by the most formidable combination of conservationists ever to cooperate in a matter of this kind in New York State.

The heart of the court action rests upon Section 432 of the Conservation Law, which says that the term "regulating reservoir" in the constitution shall not be interpreted to mean a reservoir "constructed for power purposes."

The board has publicly stated, at a joint legislative hearing in Albany, that "the primary purpose of the reservoir is power." More recently, the board has attempted to feature the Panther dam for its flood control values, although Senator Walter Stokes—chairman of the New York State Flood Control Commission—has declared himself "unalterably opposed" to this dam.

The identical people who have been called the chief beneficiaries of this flood control have signed petitions against the reservoirs and have appeared to testify against the Panther dam at the Watertown hearing. The most notable group in this category is the Black River Flats Landowners Association. Their program calls for dredging of the sandbars in the Black River and the installation of flood gates in the Carthage dam.

It should be noted that there is a drop of but nine feet in the Black River from Lyons Falls to the Carthage dam—a distance of twenty-eight miles. In addition, several rivers with poorly forested watersheds flow into the Black River from the Tug Hill Plateau in this same area. These rivers are not of the characteristics of the Moose River and its tributaries, which have heavily forested watersheds. Also, the spring snow and ice breakup on the Moose River usually does not come until a week or two after the flood peak of the Black River has been reached. This is due in part to the higher, colder altitude of the Adirondack Plateau, as against the more open and lower altitudes of the Tug Hill region which lies west of the Black River and east of Lake Ontario.

Perhaps the most important work relating to the Panther dam is document No. 405 of the 77th United States Congress. Made by the U.S. Army Engineers, it lists but 16 percent flood control for this dam, as against 84 percent power.

There are numerous places on the Black River watershed where dams might be constructed without in any way interfering with the forest preserve or the Adirondack Park. One of these sites, Hawkinsville, is a genuine flood control possibility and is listed as such on the plan of the Black River Board. But it does not have the power potentialities of Panther and would not yield power-profit commensurate with this first choice. The Adirondack Moose River Committee is on public record favoring this dam, which is within twenty-five miles of the Panther site and is located on the Black River.

It is abundantly clear that this devastation of the Adirondacks as proposed must be halted by whatever means required to do the job. Reasonable curbs upon the arbitrary powers of the Black River Board is a fundamental requisite, but even more important is an enlightened state policy which envisions an Adirondack Park so inviting that the economic value of it to the state and its people will transcend the limited economic returns to a favored few as contemplated in the proposed Panther dam.

This issue was once thrust upon the late Governor Alfred E. Smith. With typical vision and understandable language, he declared:

> The pretense of preserving the public interest is no safeguard against the private exploitation of the Adirondack Preserve. We have protected our forest preserve by constitutional safeguards for a great many years, to the great advantage of our people. A departure from this wise policy will, in my opinion, mean the eventual surrender of an important part of the state's domain wrested from destruction at great cost to the state . . .
>
> We owe it not only to ourselves but to the generations to come that the Adirondack Preserve be kept the property of all the people of this state, and should any part of it be flooded, the floodings should be restricted to the public benefit now set forth in the constitution and not for exploitation by private interests.

A Last Citadel of the Wilderness

The Moose River Plains are situated north of the West Canada Lakes and south of the Fulton Chain of Lakes in the southwestern portion of the Adirondack Park. They are accessible from many directions, the most popular trail beginning at Limekiln Lake near Inlet on the Fulton Chain and heading generally in a southeasterly direction. This trail passes Fawn Lake, climbs a spur of Seventh Lake Mountain and descends into the Red River valley. A short distance beyond the Red River the trail enters a grand spruce forest, threads through a mountain notch, and drops into the valley of the South Branch of the Moose River. This is about ten miles from Limekiln Lake. Crossing Benedict brook and the Sumner stream, the trail reaches the Great Plains where long, sweeping vistas of wild open land converge with dark evergreen forests and the gently sloping hills surrounding this unique plateau. Over and above the spruce and hardwoods may be seen an occasional giant pine, its storm-bent crown high above the spires of lesser conifers.

The Great Plains and the Little Plains close by are an entity in themselves, even though they lack the magnificence of the adjacent country. Comprising nearly seven hundred acres at an elevation of about 1850 feet, they are of a sandy composition with dips and hollows twenty to forty feet below their general mean level. Peninsulas of trees reach out from the surrounding forest and in places reach clear across the otherwise open meadows. An occasional oasis of evergreens occurs and in places these are almost impenetrable. Between the Great and the Little Plains, there is a thin strip of evergreen forest. Many years ago this forest was hit by winds of hurricane velocity, which tumbled trees

Reprinted from *Bulletin to the Schools: Arbor and Wild Life Day Issues*, University of the State of New York, March 1948, Vol. 34, No. 7, by permission of New York State Education Department.

Moose River Plains, 1946. The Moose River Plains is a unique semiopen gently undulating land surrounded by heavy forest. It is cut by the river and contains two gemlike glacial lakes. More than a thousand deer winter in this area, the largest winter-yarding ground of its kind in the northeast.

in every direction. Here and there a giant tree stands in mute testimony to individual strength but the forest, as such, is ragged and forlorn, adding a strange wildness to the scene. Within this general area, however, are to be found two small glacial lakes of rare beauty. The smallest, Icehouse Pond, is deep and cold and famous for its trout. The larger, Helldiver Pond, is shallow and in its own way is very interesting.

Close by, due north, are the Mitchell ponds. To the northeast are the Lost Ponds, which nestle in a pine forest near the Sumner still water. To the east are many miles of fine trail leading out along the old Moose River trail to Little Moose Lake near Cedar River Flow. The West Canada Lakes are about eight miles to the south. Southwest are Beaver and Squaw lakes in the magnificent Indian River country.

The trail to the Indian River region is one not easily forgotten. Proceeding on the main trail leading across the western end of the plains, it crosses the South Branch of the Moose and climbs a heavily forested ridge. Here one comes in close contact with huge white pines, some of them four feet and more in diameter and 150 feet tall. Although interspersed rather infrequently among the dominating spruces, hemlocks and hardwoods, these pines are the feature and the glory of this part of the state forest preserve.

Slightly less than two miles from the plains, the trail drops rather sharply to Beaver Lake. Its shoreline is notable, with an unbroken wall of pines, spruce, and tamarack sharply defining its peltlike shape. Its east end has a shallow sandy beach that is a favorite spot for deer and other animals during the summer months.

Beyond Beaver Lake, the best trails are made by wood folk. One of these skirts along the northern shore to the outlet and leads on down the valley to the Indian River, which is less than a mile farther on.

There may be regions equally fascinating elsewhere in the Adirondacks. It is doubtful, however, that the qualities of primitive beauty existing in this area can be surpassed anywhere in the East. The type of scenery can not be compared with Avalanche Pass, for example, for it is totally different in character. But it does have, in its own way, inspirational qualities generally associated only with such stupendous scenes as are found in the Avalanche or the Indian passes in the High Peaks region.

To follow the river upstream is to find increasingly beautiful vistas slowly unfolding. For perhaps a mile the river is a series of riffle and rapid, with occasional pools suggesting the certainty of trout. The climax of the Indian River is reached perhaps a mile and a quarter from the Moose River.

Here one looks upon a long, silver still water. The forest seems like a canyon, with spruces and balsams rising clifflike above the water and occasional giant pines dominating it all. The banks are lush with ferns and mosses and waist-high grasses. Well-worn deer paths skirt the water's edge. The river is deep here and the banks pitch off sharply.

It is a land of solitude and of antiquity. It is an open book, in which the Adirondacks of 1850 or 1750 or 1650 may be examined at will and with leisure. One might think of it as the Primitive Wing of an unchartered Museum of America, in which the background and the details have not been arranged by man. In this vast theater of the out-of-doors one may view a remnant of original America in all her moods and subtle changes. Here, according to day and season, one may watch a steady rain being absorbed in spongelike duff, to be released later in tiny springs and crystal streams which ultimately make the river. Here one can watch a great antlered buck come out of the evergreens to drink from the river, or possibly see a black bear lumber down a well-worn trail. Here also will be seen native trout jumping for flies, or a great blue heron standing statue-like on a shallow sandbar. And the deepening shadows of today's twilight will gently erase the same galaxy of color and beauty of form as in another age long since past and almost forgotten.

This is the Moose River region. In a lifetime, a man could not fully know or understand its labyrinth of trails, streams, swamps, waters, and mountains. It is a land much too big for that. It is a land that challenges exploration and invites study.

To preserve this land in its natural wild state is to bequeath to the youth of tomorrow a heritage of incalculable value; for the combination of forests, waters, and wildlife as presently contained in this Moose River region is a combination that is vanishing swiftly from America.

Sunlight and Shadow on the Moose River

We were camped among the great pines near the junction of the Indian with the South Branch of the Moose River. The night was dark, with no moon, but the stars hung like bright lanterns above the cliffs of Mount Tom and cast blue-green reflections on the deep pool below us. All was still, save for the occasional movement of wind in the lofty treetops or the rustle of woodfolk in the brush beyond the flickering firelight. Of course there was the murmuring of the river—but the music of running water is part of the silence of wild places, like the melody which fills one's mind as he walks down a winding trail into the wilderness. Here were solitude and tranquillity and peace in their most perfect form, for there is a consciousness of perfection in the form and ageless beauty of land still in the grip of the primeval influence.

On such a night it is pleasant just to be alive. And when one's companion is also of the wilderness, a few words suffice and volumes unspoken are understood. The embers had nearly burned out when we turned to the problems of the woods.

"Piseco Lake, Lake Pleasant, Goodnow Flow, the Kunjamuk River, Cedar River Flow, Thirteenth Lake, the Upper Hudson, the Schroon River, Boreas Ponds, Cheney Pond, the Essex Chain of Lakes, . . ."

"Those are the famous place-names about which I read. What pleasant thoughts they suggest!"

"But these are but a few of the places scheduled to be drowned out like this Higley basin."

"Impossible!"

"Yet, true!"

Reprinted from the *Cloudsplitter*, March–April 1949, by permission of The Cloudsplitter, Albany Chapter, ADK.

Virgin forest in the Moose River country. There was an unreality about the Higley Mountain area then. The ground on which we walked—deep, rich organic duff built up over the centuries—and the magnificent trees, which crowned the land, were quite unreal. Soon the trees would fall before the ax, fire would consume the debris, and the work of nature for thousands of years would be no more.

There was an unreality about the Higley Mountain area then. The ground on which we walked, deep, rich organic duff built by the centuries, felt strangely insecure; and the magnificent trees that crowned the land were quite unreal, for soon they would fall before the ax. Fire would consume the debris, and the work of nature for centuries would be no more! We slept uneasily that night!

The weeks and months and years that followed brought a succession of minor successes and major defeats in the effort to head off disaster in the Moose River Plains region. The final battle was won in the court of public opinion, which finally sustained the plea of the people. On November 13, 1947, the governor called for the abandonment of the Higley dam. On February 3, 1948, the official act wiping this proposed reservoir from the map of the Black River Regulating District was accomplished by the State Water Power and Control Commission.

That job is done.

But what of Panther Mountain reservoir? What of Piseco Lake reservoir? Of Cedar River Flow, of the Kunjamuk River, of Lake Pleasant?

If the river-regulating boards determined to exercise their prerogatives fully and proposed to construct their more than thirty reservoirs at one time, such a violent clamoring would arise from the people as to cause political powers to withdraw the proposals. There is no shadow of doubt about that! But what of the program to build these reservoirs one at a time? The ultimate effect would be identically the same, yet this slow process might not sufficiently shock the sensibilities of the people to cause demand for abandonment of the program.

The need for flood control by various methods is fully recognized. There can be little question that some reservoirs are justified and that river-regulating boards can and should function in a manner consistent with good conservation. This concept recognizes the broad principles of the highest use of our natural resources for the benefit of the people.

No public park in the nation is needed or used more than the Adirondack Park. It has within three hundred miles of it more than fifty million people, many of whom now benefit in one form or another from this great recreational area. We should take steps to insure that the park is protected and secured for them and for those who are to come after us.

How can this be done?

The people in 1913 approved an amendment to the constitutional "wild forest" clause, permitting the legislature to enact laws to flood up to 3 percent of state land in these mountains "for municipal water

supply, for the canals of the state, and to regulate the flow of streams."
In defining the regulation of the flow of streams, the legislature stipu-
lated that this must be done for the public health and safety, and not
for power purposes. The Black River Regulating District Board has
made power the primary objective. The Hudson River Regulating District Board has limited its activities to flood control.

It would seem that the logical way to insure proper protection
of the Adirondack lowlands would be for the people to recapture the
right they gave the legislature, by amending Section 2 of Article XIV of
the New York State Constitution, making it mandatory that the people
approve reservoirs specifically, as they do ski trails, roads, and other developments in the forest preserve.

Further, it is time that we start thinking of land within the park
as Adirondack land, rather than of just forest preserve land or private
land. What is today private land may tomorrow be forest preserve land.
It all has a critical relationship to the park in its entirety.

The job to accomplish amending Section 2 of Article XIV is a stupendous undertaking when knowledge of the opposing forces is realized. But is the job more stupendous than the task which faced the original drafters of Article VII, Section 7? What have we done in recent
years to compare with that initial job? Are not our friends legion? Do
they not include virtually all of our out-of-door groups and many civic
associations? Do not these same people elect governors and senators
and assemblymen?

Let us face the issue squarely, not be discouraged if temporary defeats are sustained during the course of the battle.

For we will remember a trail leading over a mountain to a land of
solitude and tranquillity, where cold, pure rivers run like quicksilver between avenues of trees, and glacial lakes gem forest and plain. There we
can watch deer feeding on lily pads and see lynx tracks embedded in the
sandy beach. We can watch the sunlight filter through the branches of
the cathedral-like pines to a forest floor bedecked with ferns and flowers and mosses of the wilderness.

Then, having remembered, we will become strong in the belief
that, as in the Higley Mountain question, the difference between sunlight and shadow is determination, and that the will of the people, if
fully expressed, must prevail.

Moose River

FRONTIER OF DECISION

February 3, 1948, will long be remembered as a historic date in the colorful saga of the Adirondacks, for on that day the State Water Power and Control Commission made two decisions of far-reaching consequence to the wild forest character of the New York State Forest Preserve.

The first action of the commission, of which Conservation Commissioner Perry Duryea is chairman, gave conservationists a complete and sweeping victory insofar as the proposed Higley Mountain reservoir on the South Branch of the Moose River is concerned. This proposed reservoir which had been previously approved and was about ready for construction, was stricken from the official plan of the Black River Regulating District, thus eliminating the necessity of a third attempt to outlaw this proposal by means of legislation.

The second action by the commission gave conservationists reason for grave concern, for tentative plans were approved for Panther Mountain reservoir, about twelve miles farther downstream. This approval was given despite overwhelming public opinion expressed against the dam and in the face of serious doubts raised as to the constitutionality of using forest preserve lands for power purposes. The official request for approval contained a stipulation allocating only 25 percent of the 12-billion-cubic-foot capacity for flood control.

Section 430 of Article VII of the Conservation Law states that "The term regulation reservoir . . . is not intended to include a reservoir created by a dam for power purposes."

Opposition to the Panther Mountain reservoir was reiterated at the annual statewide meeting of the Adirondack Moose River Commit-

Reprinted from the *Adirondac*, 1949, by permission of the Adirondack Mountain Club.

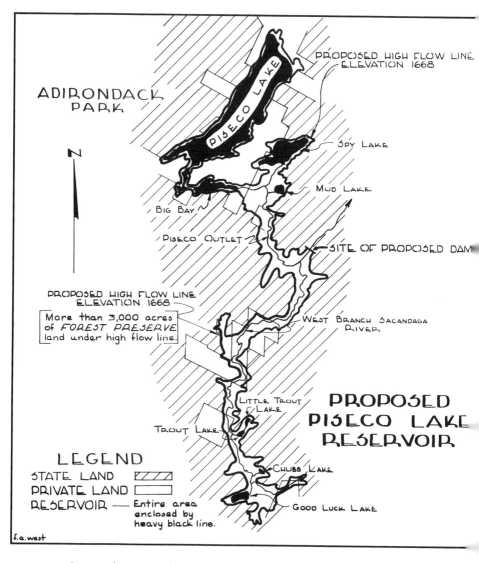

Proposed Piseco Lake Reservoir. One of scores of reservoirs eliminated by the Ostrander constitutional amendment.

tee in Utica on January 24 of this year. A few days later the State Water Power and Control Commission held a conference in Albany at which those interested in the question could be heard. As usual, the hearing was preponderantly oppositionist. It brought the conservative Association for the Protection of the Adirondacks into the front line attacking the reservoir, and found expressions of continued opposition from the powerful New York State Conservation Council and the innumerable state and national associations comprising the committee.

The problem of possible flooding of the Moose River is one which, with the master plan of the river regulating districts gradually coming into focus, has caused consternation among those who have felt that the forest preserve generally was secure from fluctuating reservoirs created for economic purposes.

To think of the problem of flooding the river basins in the Adirondacks as isolated reservoirs, such as Panther, rather than to grasp the picture of scores of completed reservoirs located in the choice river and lake regions of these mountains, is to be blind to the mortal danger these developments are to the natural wild character of the forest preserve.

Reservoirs, some very large and others relatively small, have been mapped for the following well known place names in the Adirondacks, and this list is by no means complete: Piseco Lake, Lake Pleasant, Goodnow Flow, Cedar River Flow, Elm Lake and in the Kunjamuk country, Thirteenth Lake, Boreas Ponds, Cheney Ponds, the Upper Hudson River, the Schroon River, Indian Lake, and the Essex Chain of Lakes.

We should be realistic enough to understand that a reservoir such as the Sacandaga is a necessary flood control project and that there may be other areas where similar conditions exist and where important economic, recreational, and wildlife values would not be lost by such flooding.

We should also be realistic enough to see this whole problem in its true perspective and understand that unless we change the blueprint of construction as it is now laid before us, much of the heart of Adirondack wild land will be irrevocably lost.

A constitutional provision limits to 3 percent the amount of forest preserve land which can be flooded for the public health and safety. It does not say that any quantity of available private land can be flooded, although of course it can be, nor is it generally realized that this relatively small percentage of land is indeed large enough to permit flooding of all the good river basin reservoir sites existing in these mountains.

This is the time for decision.

Perhaps it will require a constitutional amendment eliminating the three percent clause in Section 2 of Article XIV. This will require a long and sustained battle, but victory is not inconceivable. Perhaps a statutory provision requiring the legislature to pass on these available sites would do the job. Perhaps the impending Supreme Court action on Panther, in itself a very costly move which must be assumed by interested people, will clear the air and indicate a definite course of procedure.

We have the choice of looking down from September mountaintops upon dreary mud flats, drowned forests and lost rivers, or, if we will, upon lovely, lush valleys where crystal rivers thread between canyons of trees and glacial lakes reflect, as they have for centuries, such wild-forest scenes as are synonymous with the word "Ad-i-ron-dac."

We who profess fidelity to this chosen land cannot ignore the challenge before us. The job is clearly defined; let's get going!

Why the Ostrander Committee Succeeded

Students of Adirondack history years hence may wonder about the combination of statesmanship and political strategy which made possible the legislative success of the recommendation (Amendment No. 9 to Article XIV, Section 2, of the New York State Constitution) of the Joint Legislative Committee on River Regulation for New York State under the chairmanship of Assemblyman John L. Ostrander.

Before introduction of the proposed amendment in the 1952 session of the New York State Legislature, it had already been defeated three times, in 1949, 1950, and 1951. What magic was used to enable it to win decisively in 1952 and 1953?

There was no magic. But there was a terrific amount of hard work on the part of a lot of people. And there was real statesmanship on the part of many public leaders.

Assemblyman Ostrander started his job in an extremely businesslike way. He called the first meeting of his committee in the Adirondacks and studied the Higley and Panther mountain reservoir proposals firsthand. That was in 1949.

Then he called a series of public hearings over a period of two years and built up a public record almost unparalleled in legislative history. At the first public hearing in Schenectady in 1949, conservationist leaders frankly told the committee that they did not know the answer to the committee's problems. But as the hearings progressed to Buffalo, Watertown, Albany, Cranberry Lake, and New York City, the solution became more and more apparent.

As the nation's foremost conservationists testified, public leaders were making up their minds. New York State Comptroller Frank C.

Reprinted from the *Forest Preserve*, March 1954.

Assemblyman John Ostrander *(standing)*, chairman of the Joint
Legislative Committee on River Regulation for New York State, at
a public hearing with national conservation leaders in New York
City. Photograph courtesy of NYS Department of Environmental
Conservation.

Moore, in a dramatic, unannounced appearance before the committee
in Buffalo before he was elected lieutenant governor, gave voice to
thoughts which have since echoed throughout the state. He said: "I am
wholeheartedly in favor of a constitutional amendment which will grant
to the people of this state the right to approve or reject in referendum
proposals to construct reservoirs in the Adirondack Park."

This position had previously been taken by Assembly Speaker
Oswald D. Heck in Watertown, but Mr. Moore's statement dramatized
the issue and brought it before the people as it had not been before.

United States Senator Herbert H. Lehman, Richard J. Balch, William L. Pheiffer, and leaders of both major political parties gave needed
support. Senator Francis Mahoney and Assemblyman Eugene Bannigan,

minority leaders in their respective houses, staked their leadership on support of the amendment which was opposed by important segments of labor and big business. Majority Leader Arthur H. Wicks and other key legislators kept faith with the people they represented.

The success of the Ostrander Committee, then, was based on these sound foundations:

1. The committee personally inspected many reservoir sites and examined in detail the extent of possible destruction they would cause to the forest preserve.

2. Members of the committee personally waded rivers, climbed mountains, and studied forest and watershed conditions in the Adirondacks.

3. The committee obtained a true picture of the facts, and of public reaction by holding public hearings wherever they were requested. One hearing in New York City brought twenty-five of the foremost conservationists of the nation, including representatives of the United States Forest, Fish and Wildlife, and Soil Conservation Services and many others.

4. Upon reaching a decision, prompted by the merits of the case, the committee courageously fought for its convictions against strong odds and came out on top, overwhelmingly, because it was right!

The People of New York State

represented by the undersigned conservationists in conference at the Edison Club, Schenectady, New York, July 11, 1953, are pleased to confer upon

Honorable John L. Ostrander

Chairman, Joint Legislative Committee on River Regulation for New York State, this expression of appreciation for the vision, statesmanship and courage he has evidenced during the period 1949-1953. As Chairman of this bi-partisan joint legislative committee, he successfully guided through the Legislature of 1952 and 1953 an amendment to Section 2 of Article XIV of the New York State Constitution which will preserve from destruction by reservoirs the river valleys and lake basins of the New York State Forest Preserve in the Adirondack and Catskill Mountains.

These words cannot adequately express our appreciation, but the rivers and the lakes, the forests and wildlife protected by this action will remain forever as living tribute to the determination of his Committee and of the New York State Legislature to maintain for the people and posterity the wild forest character of the N.Y. State Forest Preserve in the Adirondacks and Catskills. Inscribed this 11th day of July 1953 by

[signature]
President, N.Y. State Conservation Council

[signature]
President, Adirondack Moose River Committee

[signature]
President, Friends of the Forest Preserve

[signature]
President, Mohawk Hudson Federation of Conservation Councils

[signature]
Isaak Walton League of America

[signature]
President, Schenectady County Conservation Council

and, in behalf of the hundreds of citizens assembled here today either officially representing women's garden clubs, labor organizations, farm or service clubs or attending as individuals.

[signature]
President, Association for the Protection of the Adirondacks

A Banquet

The Ostrander Amendment sets up no impassable barrier to the use of forest preserve land for any purpose. What would be established by its passage is the principle that in matters of such grave importance the legislature shall be consulted and shall be given ample time to reach a wise decision. I say that is right. I know you agree. I have not the slightest shadow of a doubt that the people of the state will also agree." Thus did Lithgow Osborne, conservation commissioner during the period from 1933 to 1942 and currently president of the Association for the Protection of the Adirondacks, open the campaign for Amendment No. 9 at a banquet honoring Assemblyman John L. Ostrander, Senator John H. Cooke, and members of the New York State Legislature at the Edison Club in Schenectady, on July ll.

More than four hundred men and women from fifty-three counties of our state's sixty-two were on hand to express to the legislators their thanks for a job well done, and to begin serious planning for the battle at the polls this fall. Considering the vacation season and the usual difficulty of getting a really representative group of leaders out, the turnout was amazing. It was a great tribute to the legislative leaders and indicated the devotion of our people to efforts made in behalf of the forest preserve.

Lieutenant Governor Frank C. Moore, Senator Francis Mahoney, Democratic State Chairman Richard H. Balch, Donald M. Tobey, Vermont's Conservation Commissioner George W. Davis, Robert Thompson, president of the New York State Conservation Council, Allen Potter, president of the Izaak Walton League and Herman Forster, president of the Adirondack Moose River Committee were at the speakers' table. Leaders of all regional county federations were on hand, together with officers from more than fifty county councils. Numerous noted

Reprinted from the *Forest Preserve*, March 1954.

women conservationists attended, among them Rosalie Edge, Mary Slifer, Grace Hudowalski, Elsie B. Darbee, and Mrs. David Prince. Karl T. Frederick, Dr. Morris Mandel Cohn, Russell M. L. Carson, Richard Pough, the Conservation Department's Director of Lands and Forests William M. Foss, Senators Wheeler Milmoe and Gilbert Seelye, Assemblymen Robert Watson Pomeroy, Archibald Douglas, and numerous labor leaders, members of farm organizations and service clubs were also on hand.

More than a hundred wires and letters of regret were received from many of the most outstanding conservationists in the state and nation.

Victory on the Moose River

On November 8, 1955, the people of New York State decisively defeated the proposed amendment to Article XIV of the state constitution which would have permitted construction of Panther Mountain dam on the South Branch of the Moose River. The vote was 1,622,196 to 613,927.

Thus has ended one of the longest and most costly conservation battles in history. It has also been the most productive for its effect on many other issues concerning the New York State Forest Preserve.

The lovely valley of the South Branch of the Moose River near the heart of the Adirondack Park begins at Little Moose Lake and stretches westerly to McKeever about thirty miles distant. Because of this vote, this valley shall not become a vast millpond fluctuating at the will of downstream power interests, nor shall its abundant wildlife be lost, its forests and plains become dreary mud flats, or its lovely lakes destroyed. And now that the proposed Higley Mountain impoundment has also become the target of an aroused public, the splendid natural conditions of this unique region shall continue to flourish as they have for so many ages past. And youth, in distant tomorrows, will be able to backpack the trail past Fawn Lake, down the Red River to the Moose River Plains and beyond to the virgin Beaver Lake and Indian River country. There they will find, as we have, the remoteness, the solitude, and all the riches inherent in wilderness.

The Panther-Higley dam battles took on a new life on September 25, 1945. On that day a brochure entitled *The Impending Tragedy of the Moose River Region* was mailed from Schenectady to newspapers statewide and to the relatively few conservationists we were acquainted with at that time. Up to then the issue, although developing for decades,

Friends of the Forest Preserve brochure, December 1955.

Oasis on the Moose River Plains. Shall the Adirondack Park lose its wild-forest character to lumbering, which will yield doubtful remuneration to the state?

had not caught the public attention. Those most intimately involved in the issue had all but given up hope of blocking the impoundments proposed by the Black River Regulating District Board and approved by state agencies.

Ed Richard of Fort Plain and Allen Wilcox of Fourth Lake first supplied us with basic information about the proposals. They arranged a flight for me over the region.

From the sky, I could see forests unlimited, dotted with the crowns of giant white pines. Crystal lakes sparkling in the sunshine. The Moose River threading through the open plains and into the deep woods westerly. Trails twisting along tributary streams down towards the river. And in the distance, range on range of mountains, fading into far horizons. Unspoiled wilderness everywhere!

The very thought that all this marvelous country would be devastated was the catalyst that moved us all down that long road which ended the other day—November 8th—ten years and forty-four days later.

But at that time, ten years ago, the final order approving the Higley impoundment upstream from Panther had been signed and heavy equipment was being mobilized to start construction.

One of the definitions of the word *impoundment* is "to seize and retain legal custody." The power interests would take *our* forest preserve, *our* lakes and streams, *our* wildlife haven for their commercial purposes?

The battle started. It began as isolated skirmishes, gradually increasing in tempo as the public became aware of the issues. As newspapers took up the question, more and more people became involved. An Adirondack Moose River Committee was formed, mobilizing the best fighting abilities of the New York State Conservation Council, the Izaak Walton League, the Association for the Protection of the Adirondacks, the Adirondack Mountain Club, the Forest Preserve Association, the Friends of the Forest Preserve, and many more. Service clubs, garden clubs, labor groups, and churches all joined hands. The Wilderness Society, the Wildlife Management Institute, the National Parks Association, the American Nature Association and the Emergency Conservation Committee. All these and more.

Who can count the men, the women, and the youth who contributed their time and talents to the fight since that fateful day in 1945?

Ed Richard was a dynamo. Herman Forster, Karl Frederick, Lee Keator, Martha Benedict, John Apperson, Don Tobey, Bob Thompson, Mike Petruska, Bob Young, Ira Gabrielson, Howard Zahniser, Anthony

Wayne Smith—one after the other, they joined the fray, adding resources unprecedented. Assembly Speaker Oswald Heck, Lieutenant Governor Frank Moore, Assemblymen Leo Lawrence, Justin Morgan, John Ostrander, Senators Francis Mahoney, Chauncey Hammond, Walter Stokes—one after the other became allies. And of major influence was our public relations chief, Fred Smith of New York.

Legal action began early with Milo Kniffen and Judge Walter Bliss, the forerunners of a score of brilliant lawyers who pooled their expertise. Timothy Cohan, assistant attorney general, Sanford Stockton of the Adirondack League Club and, Mayor Curtis Frank of Yonkers, were among them. Thousands of pages of briefs were submitted to the Supreme Court and the Court of Appeals.

Traveling became a way of life, with business responsibilities for many put in the background. New York City, Buffalo, Rochester, Syracuse, Utica, Binghamton, Kingston, Morrisville, Brownville, Broadalbin, Cobleskill, Albany, Jamestown, Waverly. And hundreds more cities and towns. Movies and slides to overflow audiences. Billboards on highways. Doug's Roughriders—youth on horseback—delivering pamphlets to remote rural areas. Television spots. Newspaper ads. And, on the last day, sportsmen in outdoor wear at hundreds of voting booths, at legal distances, urging the negative vote. A vote that became positive overnight and the rallying cry to save the Adirondacks from commercial exploitation!

After many legislative failures and numerous court injunctions to hold the line, the Stokes Act of 1950 banned dams on the Moose River. In 1953 the Ostrander constitutional amendment banned all dams "to regulate the flow of streams" in the Adirondacks if they involved the forest preserve. A special amendment to build Panther Mountain dam had been passed by the legislature.

It seems incredible that even with all this help, we were able to pull back from the brink of disaster that marvelous Moose River country. We have been on the defensive too long. It is time to gather our forces and to accomplish things that heretofore have been but dreams.

4

The Upper Hudson

Upper Hudson River. "The river is the refuge for the spirit of man. Any move to dam its water, free-flowing for centuries, must be stopped!" — Peter Paine, 1973.

The mineral that hampered the commercial exploitation of the iron deposits on the Upper Hudson near Tahawus was titanium, a substance critical for many industrial uses. The major producer of that mineral early in World War II was India. Submarines threatened to cut off that supply. Realizing there was a major titanium deposit in the Adirondacks, the United States defense department moved quickly to exploit it. First they improved the highway system and then built a railroad on forest preserve land despite objections and a law suit by the State of New York to prevent it.

Soon the Tahawus region became a major industrial center. Buildings and refineries were constructed, and an all-out twenty-four-hour-a-day work schedule was set up. Soon a mountain was being leveled, Sanford Lake destroyed and the Upper Hudson River in that region absolutely ruined. But there was a problem much larger than the visual one. In my article in the *Adirondac*, I noted the pollution in the river and decried it. The New York State Conservation Department contacted me and suggested that I file a complaint with the state attorney general. This I did, and the response was immediate. The conservation department was asked to make a biological survey of the river and report back to the attorney general.

Biologist Dr. George Burdick contacted me and arranged for Ed Richard and me to meet him and an assistant at Tahawus the next week. This we did. We made camp on the river bank several miles below the mine, which we quickly observed was pouring its entire residue waste directly into the river. It was black with mine tailings.

We determined to test the damage by fishing and examining those caught. We found no serious effects on such fish; Ed and I began to wonder at the correctness of our complaint. Then the biologists told us that particulates were found much farther south in the river's mouth at Manhattan. They said that if this situation was to continue, over a period of time the bottom of the river would become as dead of aquatic life as a concrete highway.

When this report got to the attorney general he issued an order to the mining company to desist immediately, to provide a holding basin for its tailings, and to see to it that the river was protected.

The company complied, and soon the river was relatively clear again. And the holding basin kept hundreds of thousands of tons of particulates from destroying aquatic and fish life in the Upper Hudson.

Another major threat to the Upper Hudson surfaced in 1965. It was proposed that a huge dam block off the Hudson River either near Kettle Mountain or near private land leased by the Gooley Club at the junction of the Indian River and the Hudson, just below the confluence of the fabled Cedar River. The dam would cause the destruction of fifteen thousand acres of forest, drown out numerous lovely river valleys, and extend thirty-five miles north to envelop the town of Newcomb, inundate portions of the eighteen-thousand-acre Huntington Wildlife Forest of Syracuse University, and obliterate Lake Harris and Rich Lake. It was an absolutely incredible proposal, being actively pushed by the United States Army Corps of Engineers, the City of New York, and certain state agencies. Because the project was proposed as a reservoir for "municipal water supply," which was permitted under the constitution, the issue took on a very serious aspect. The reservoir proposed would be more damaging to the integrity of the Adirondack Park than would have been Panther Mountain dam, for this proposal would have flooded out the geographic heart of the park.

An Adirondack Hudson River Association was immediately formed along the general lines of the Adirondack Moose River Committee. We decided early that the only way we could kill this proposal would be a major statewide educational campaign with our ultimate goal to attain an act of the legislature specially prohibiting the dam, similar to the Stokes Act of 1950 which banned any dams on the Moose River.

We managed to get public hearings called to publicize our position and hear the arguments of the proponents; we began work on a documentary motion picture which was a powerful advocate for our side; and we began to line up key statesmen and other public leaders to support our position. In this we were successful, getting immediate support from men like Senator Bernard Smith, Senator Robert Watson Pomeroy, Laurance S. Rockefeller, and many others. The key legislator in this phase of the effort was Assemblyman Glenn Harris who represented an Adirondack constituency.

Our experience in the Moose River fight was, of course, fundamental to our growing success. The big organizations, still heady from the Panther Mountain success, backed us strongly. Most of the newspapers, which were reluctant to back us in the earlier days, readily came to our support this time.

We called two major conferences, one at the North Woods Club in 1969 and the other at the Newcomb High School in 1970 which overflowed with more than seven hundred people, all violently against Gooley or Kettle Mountain dams.

Legislation was not an easy matter. Senator Smith introduced the bill we proposed that was based on the Stokes Act of 1950, but it languished in the senate for political reasons. Then one day an amazing break came which substantially settled the issue. It came about this way.

We had no reading of any kind from the assembly of which Stanley Steingut was the minority leader. One night I met a friend of his in Albany, and I explained our dilemma to him. "When do you want to see Stanley?" he asked. "As soon as possible," I replied. "How about Monday morning?" he asked. It was Saturday night. I doubted his ability to make such a hasty arrangement.

"You be in the waiting room of his office at 9:00 A.M. sharp. You don't need confirmation. Just be there!" he told me.

I was there, fifteen minutes early. The room was already filled with people waiting to see Mr. Steingut. I questioned my sanity for even thinking I could see such a busy person on the issue. But promptly at 9:00 A.M. the door opened, and a secretary called my name. "Mr. Schaefer, Mr. Steingut will see you," she said.

Dumbfounded, I went in. Steingut sat at his desk and motioned me to a chair. "I understand you knew my father," he said. I acknowledged that I did and that his father and Senator Herbert Lehman had combined forces to help us win the Panther Mountain fight. He had me tell him about it. There was no sense of time pressure in our interview. Then he asked me what he could do. I told him that Senator Bernard C. Smith had told me Friday that he could not move our bill to ban Gooley dam because he could get no commitment from the Democratic house. He assured me that if he had such a commitment he could get enough Republican votes to pass the bill.

Steingut smiled, "Go up and tell Bernie that I have promised you every Democratic vote in the assembly." I shook his hand and headed for Senator Smith's office. He told me he was still stymied for lack of word from the assembly. Then I told him about Steingut's statement. He was amazed but immediately dialed Mr. Steingut's office. Steingut assured him that it was true.

Several days later, the bill to ban any dam on the Upper Hudson was passed by the senate 53-0 and by the assembly 121-0. Perry B. Duryea, speaker of the assembly, provided the Republican votes that made the opposition against the dam unanimous.

Another four-year battle was over when the bill was signed by the governor a few days later.

These actions spawned the Wild, Scenic, and Recreational Rivers bill that Senator Smith proposed in the senate and Assemblyman Glenn Harris in the assembly.

The Tragedy of the Hudson

The Hudson River has always symbolized the beauty and the romance of the Adirondacks. Rising on the precipitous heights of Mount Marcy, its sparkling waters drop more than a thousand feet from Lake Tear-of-the-Clouds to the valley of Lakes Avalanche and Colden and the Flowed Lands. Here the Opalescent River tumbles over Hanging Spear Falls and rushes down through a rugged, boulder-stream valley to a point just below Sanford Lake. Here also is formed Calamity Brook which joins the Henderson River just below Calamity Pond and eventually forms Sanford Lake in Tahawus valley. The river becomes of age here and flows on down through the picturesque central Adirondacks.

Famed for its native and rainbow trout and its black bass, the river has always been the delight of fishermen, campers, and hikers who drank of its pure waters and dove in its deep, cool pools. Its wooded shores, particularly in the Sanford Lake valley, probably sheltered more deer than any similar area in the north woods.

It seems incredible that all these things which have enriched the lives of so many of our people are now threatened with permanent destruction as a result of mining operations in Tahawus valley.

The other day, I stood on the bridge where the Roosevelt-Marcy highway crosses the Hudson. The river, no longer crystal-clear, was black and the rocks and the banks were covered with a thick, claylike coating. Later I stood in the fire observation tower on Mount Adams and looked southward towards the valley we once loved so well. I listened to the rumble of machinery on the open-pit mine at Sanford Lake, no longer a gem of the north glistening in the sunlight but a black, murky sewer into which poured a never-ending stream of refuse from

Reprinted from *High Spots*, 1944, by permission of the Adirondack Mountain Club.

Dr. George Burdick *(left)* with assistant and Ed Richard *(right)* at their campsite on the Upper Hudson River, 1944. "If the pollution is allowed to continue, after a period of time the bottom of the Hudson River will become like a concrete highway, killing all aquatic and fish life" — Dr. George Burdick.

the mine. Already the lake is filled with semisolid material from shore to island. If continued the lake will become a pit of mud—a wellspring of refuse which could conceivably pollute the Hudson for years after the mining operation stopped or after the mineowners were required to dispose of their refuse by other means.

In the same area where a few years ago it was commonplace to see from ten to thirty deer any morning or evening along a ten-mile stretch of road, I failed to see any. Worse, in walking three miles along Sanford Lake I saw little evidence of any wildlife. Other reasons than pollution alone may have caused the disappearance of the deer herds; on the other hand it is difficult to conceive of animals drinking or living near such water.

The importance of the Sanford Lake region's minerals for war purposes is admitted but the necessity for the destruction of this world-famous scenery and recreation land can never be admitted. Other methods of disposing of the refuse of the mines surely can be devised, if indeed they are not already available but perhaps more costly.

Lack of adequate laws governing this type of pollution is the explanation given by state officials for not having stopped this destruction to date. Surveys are being made and conferences are being held. Meanwhile, thousands of tons of additional refuse are being dumped into the lake and river each week. It may soon be too late for action by the state. It may be like buying a mountain for the forest preserve after the soil has been consumed by fire and tree growth made impossible for a dozen centuries or so.

If existing laws are inadequate to stop this destruction, new legislation should be at once devised and offered the legislature. We have talked with prominent people in many parts of the state, and there is no question but that the public will strongly endorse such specific legislation.

The incredible Gooley dam proposal.

The Impending Tragedy of the
Upper Hudson Region

From its source in Lake Tear-of-the-Clouds near the summit of Mount Marcy to Luzerne at the southern boundary of the Adirondack Park, the Upper Hudson is truly one of the great wild rivers of America.

Fed by pure crystal springs and streams with innumerable cataracts and rapids draining the High Peaks of the Adirondacks, the Hudson threads a serpentine course through lovely forests and imposing mountain and cliff country for nearly a hundred miles and cascades more than three thousand feet below its source.

For generations engineers have been building huge dams and reservoirs throughout America. While it seems incredible that the Upper Hudson has been spared the fate of so many other rivers, the portion within the Adirondack Park has, to date, been permitted to remain in its natural state. There are approximately twenty dams on the Hudson, but they are outside the park.

Now, however, there is a major threat to destroy a significant portion of the Upper Hudson—a portion that includes valuable forests and lakes of the New York State Forest Preserve, a portion close to the geographical center of the Adirondack Park!

The New York State Water Resources Commission has issued an engineering report listing the proposed "Gooley No. 1 Dam" to be constructed a short distance below the confluence of the Indian River with the Hudson. Costing more than $57 million the proposed "millpond" would require 16,000 acres of land, of which 14,500 acres would be flooded. The uses of this reservoir, more than thirty-five miles long, have been listed by the commission as "municipal and industrial water

Adirondack Hudson River Association brochure, 1968.

supply, power and recreation". An amendment to Article XIV of the New York State Constitution would be necessary before construction of this reservoir, although it is understood that several members of the Water Resources Commission believe that such an amendment would be unnecessary.

Recently, in addition to the New York State Water Resources Commission report, the City of New York released a similar report which included proposals to flood this part of the Hudson. They listed four possible dam sites, all close to the "Gooley No.1" site, but some posing even more danger. They frankly admit that water levels would fluctuate more than fifty to seventy feet!

These proposals are far more destructive than the now infamous Panther Mountain dam would have been had it become a reality. To view the impending tragedy, one needs only to stand on Prospect Rock near the southern border of the North Woods Club and look out over the magnificent canyon and forested country below: there is no similar wilderness country in eastern America! The deep gorge through the wild forest, the high cliffs of the Blue Ledge, and the long sweeping valley of the Indian River surrounded by dramatically glaciated peaks, lesser mountains and hills all combine to form the kind of breathtaking scenery which must be preserved at all costs.

The Hudson from the Indian River downstream is exquisite. It is a symphony of rapids and great dark pools, of water-sculptured rock banks, and of immense overpowering cliffs. From the trails leading to the river, the roar of the rapids can be heard in the splendid forests, which include some virgin timber. The trails cross extensive winter-yarding grounds of deer and some semiopen country, excellent big game range, which was recently acquired by the state. A first glimpse of the river is one always to be remembered. It roars over boulders, swirls in great eddies and whirlpools, boils up from hidden obstructions, and rushes away untamed to the next white-water rapids. The sand bars along quieter stretches are laced with the tracks of coon and otter and bird life. Deer and bear frequent certain shores. Banks of ferns and clumps of flowers grow in unexpected profusion. Great white pines and ancient cedars crown the heavy forest which encloses the steep banks above rock cliffs. Stunted trees cling precariously to tiny ledges high in the rocks. Hawks soar in the narrow sky visible above the river. Above the cliffs and steep banks on both sides of the river, for the entire length of the proposed reservoir, are almost unbroken forests and numerous lakes and streams, many of which are state-owned. Some of the land is privately owned and usefully used and managed, while much of the land is in the New York State Forest Preserve. All of the land is rich with un-limited potential and uses for our people. Good trails penetrate the miles of rugged country between the existing state roads and the river. It is the kind of country big enough and wild enough to challenge most of us, yet it is accessible. It is the kind of country that is rapidly disap-pearing from the face of America. It is this kind of country that is needed desperately by a civilization which is rapidly becoming more re-stricted and more artificial.

New York State is blessed with water. There are more than seven thousand lakes; and more than seventy thousand miles of rivers and streams; the state is virtually surrounded by the Great Lakes, the Saint Lawrence River, Lake Champlain and other waters. But our greatest water resources—our underground supplies which comprise approxi-mately 90 percent of all of our fresh water resources—have hardly been tapped!

Our engineers can and must find water supplies elsewhere rather than destroy the irreplaceable valleys which do so much to contribute to the beauty and wealth of our state. Important breakthroughs have been made in the desalinization of sea water, a supply which is limitless. Competent engineers expect more advances in this field; at the present time they can produce water for twenty-five cents per one thousand gal-lons. It should also be kept in mind that there is a possibility that Can-ada, estimated to possess from one-seventh to one-third of all the fresh water on earth, may be willing to sell some of their virtually limitless supply to this country, as they do their ore and other natural resources.

We are not talking merely about the loss of a portion of the Upper Hudson River when we talk of the proposed reservoirs; we are talking about the destruction of the world-famous Adirondack Park! The loca-tion for this proposed project is close to the geographical center of the park. It contains some of our most spectacular scenery and some of our finest wilderness as well as some of our most economically useful lands.

To drown out Yellowstone National Park would hardly be more outrageous!

The United States Army Corps of Engineers is currently surveying the proposed reservoir. We are told that this is merely a "feasibility study," but until such time as the New York State Water Resources Commission publicly disavows this project we must assume that its construction is being seriously considered by that agency and others.

In a summary report dated 1966, the Hudson River Valley Com-mission stated: "The upper reaches of the Hudson and its tributaries are wild rivers, and the commission recommends that they be given this status by the state. Generally, this protection should be given the reaches between Luzerne and the river's source; the Boreas, the Indian from its mouth to Abanakee Dam, the Cedar from its mouth to Cedar River Flow. These reaches total about 130 miles of especially attractive stream land, all of it within the Adirondack Park." (For the record, it should be noted that the Hudson River Valley Commission has taken no official stand since release of this summary report.)

It is time to assess the fundamental requirements of all the people of our state in relation to the need for adequate water supplies. Because some municipalities pollute our rivers and streams, because some refuse to meter existing water supplies, because some allow the waste of water from antiquated and broken water mains and laterals, shall the people, as a whole, be forced to sacrifice lovely wilderness valleys and villages like Newcomb, which will be under fifty feet of water should this proposed Gooley dam be built?

Are we willing to lose the best trout waters remaining in our state, excellent big-game hunting country, and some of our very best winter-yarding grounds for deer? Shall we replace the challenging five-hour white-water canoe adventures through country federal officials have described as the "most spectacular river scenery in the East" with boating on a wildly fluctuating millpond? Shall we drown out miles of fine hiking trails and wilderness campsites, replacing them with a cemetery of stumps and dreary mud flats?

We need to take a stand on the Upper Hudson, a stand that knows no compromise, a stand that will accept no halfway effort, nor be satisfied with any engineering study less than one needed to permanently preserve the Hudson from destruction.

The Adirondack Hudson River Association, with the cooperation of virtually all conservation and sportsmen's groups in the state, has initiated action dedicated to maintaining the natural free-flowing Hudson within the Adirondack Park. We need the support of all who value the wild-forest character of the Adirondacks.

The Upper Hudson
TIME FOR DECISION

The Upper Hudson River, from the Boreas to Lake Harris some thirty miles upstream, is wild and lovely. The country through which it flows has many unique natural splendors and is abundant with challenges for the adventurous.

Close to the geographical center of the Adirondack Park, the Hudson contains an unusual combination of white-water rapids and deep, dark pools, ancient forests and imposing cliffs, towering side canyons and high waterfalls. Over the centuries, the river has cut a deep gorge through rugged mountains, and its serpentine flow has worn caves and grottoes in the base of the cliffs which hem it in. Numerous glacial lakes and crystal streams, enclosed by heavy forest, are found throughout the high plateaus hundreds of feet above the river.

The river itself is isolated from main highways by the ruggedness of this terrain, with the result that much of the wilderness character of the region has been preserved. This is deer, bear, and trout country. Here also is an abundance of smaller wildlife, including beaver, otter, fisher, and hare. Eagles are occasionally seen circling in the thin strip of sky above the canyon.

The best access to the river, of course, is by canoe. One can shove off into the Hudson just below the bridge in the community of Newcomb and for five action-filled hours run through the most spectacular river scenery in eastern America. In springtime, the river will tax the capabilities of the best white-water enthusiasts. Many of those who make the trip enjoy lingering along the way. There are numerous fine campsites which have been used by fishermen for over a century. At Blue

Reprinted from the *Conservationist*, December–January 1968–69; and from the *Living Wilderness*, Winter 1968–69, by permission of The Wilderness Society.

Blue Ledge on the Upper Hudson. After he understood the uniqueness of the region, Peter Paine *(second from left)* put his political expertise to work. He was one of the key members of state agencies who thwarted devastation of the Upper Hudson River by the proposed Gooley dam.

Ledge, there is a sunny, boulder-stream sandbar under the high cliffs. Build your campfire there with the music of untamed rapids soothing your soul and with banks of ferns and clumps of flowers in profusion around you. Great pines rim the pool, cedars cling precariously to cliff ledges, and sparkling water drips down through blankets of moss.

At Kettle Mountain there is a campsite under great pines and hemlocks close to another rapids. Here the waters of 0.K. Slip Brook, the outlet of a lake by the same peculiar name, meet and join the Hudson. Hike up this narrow side canyon, so filled with great blocks of stone broken from the cliffs that sometimes you must go under them, and you will suddenly come to its end. There dropping off an incredibly high precipice is O.K. Slip Falls, one of the loveliest waterfalls in the Adirondacks!

While there are numerous good trails to the river, an extremely interesting one starts at Huntley Pond on the North Woods Club road. Following the trail a short distance around this state-owned trout lake and southwesterly two and one-half miles the hiker will find himself at the foot of the massive cliffs at Blue Ledge. One of the truly great Adirondack experiences you can know is to see the power of the river in springtime at this place. Great boulders and hidden obstructions cause the water to fairly boil as it whirls untamed on to the next rapids. All along the river's plateau, the steady roar of the rapids can be heard; the precipitous walls of rocks and trees seem to hold within them the wildness which is the reality of this great river.

Upstream, the Indian and the Cedar rivers add their tribute to the Hudson. The former is a continuous succession of rapids and small falls; the latter, a quiet stream meandering through spired evergreen country. Goodnow Flow, Wolf Creek, and Ords Falls are also part of this great complex of woods and water.

At Lake Harris is one of the state's finest public campsites, complete with a beach and boat-launching site. Almost every campsite is right on the lake which is nearly two miles long. To the west is Rich Lake and the Huntington Wildlife Research Forest, operated by Syracuse University. This region is favored habitat for both large and small wildlife.

The Town of Newcomb is historically important to the Adirondacks. Today, Newcomb has three churches, a school, a medical center and other amenities of a modern village. All of this country, some sixteen thousand acres, would be inundated, or isolated, by the proposed reservoir—most of it by a depth of more than one hundred feet of water.

Because of the widely fluctuating nature of the proposed water impoundment, the wild-forest character of the entire central Adirondack Park would be substantially lost.

A fifty-foot drop in the water level would expose a totally destroyed forest region around Harris and Rich lakes, the river proper and the lands near the North Woods Club, so graphically painted by Winslow Homer. The lands of the Gooley Club and many favored winter yarding grounds of the deer would be obliterated forever; one hundred miles of existing river and lake frontage would be transformed into dreary mud flats. Much of the land involved is the New York State Forest Preserve, while some is privately owned but usefully managed for the benefit of many.

When we think of private lands here and elsewhere within the Adirondack Park, we should keep in mind that each citizen of New York State has an undivided interest in all 2.7 million acres of the New York State Forest Preserve. This is The People's Club—a vast heritage of mountains, lakes, rivers, and forests!

The people of the state pay equal taxes on state lands and often a very large percentage of town and county taxes. In the Upper Hudson area, the wildlife moves freely from private to state lands. In many cases, the owners of the private lands have been, to a very large extent, responsible for the gradual development of the park. In addition, they have often protected lands from devastation for long, critical periods of time when the state was financially unable to acquire them. They later sold or gave portions of their lands to the state to become part of the forest preserve. This is not to say that adjustments for better access to state lands should not be made, for adjustments are needed for the mutual benefit of all concerned. In this respect, a careful study of the Upper Hudson country should be made in line with the serious reappraisals contemplated by Governor Rockefeller's Temporary Study Commission on the Future of the Adirondacks.

The controversy as to the best ultimate use of this region is one we must face dispassionately and realistically. What are the alternatives to this impoundment? What engineering and conservation measures can be undertaken to make preservation of the Upper Hudson River possible? There are engineering and conservation measures which can adequately replace the need to drown out the Upper Hudson!

The use of water meters by all municipalities and the correction of faulty mains and laterals, in itself, could vastly increase our present supply of water. We have hardly spoken about the waters which are available in our polluted rivers and streams. We have hardly spoken about

SCHENECTADY GAZETTE

THIRD SECTION   SCHENECTADY, N.Y., 12301, THURSDAY MORNING, APRIL 17, 1969   PAGE 27

Assembly Votes 121-0 to Bar Gooley Dam

By PETE JACOBS
Gazette Reporter

ALBANY—Without opposition, the Assembly gave swift approval to legislation prohibiting the construction of the Gooley Dam on the Upper Hudson River, branded by conservationists as a threat to the wild river country.

* * *

In addition to Gooley, the bill blocks construction of any reservoirs on the river from Luzerne to its source in the Adirondack Park.

The estimated $57 million dam was proposed as a source of water supply for the long-range needs of New York City and other communities along the lower river.

Passed 121 to 0, the bill goes to the governor for his signature.

Conservation-oriented groups, including the Adirondack Hudson River Association, led by President Paul Schaefer of Schenectady, were prime opponents of the dam.

* * *

They claimed the reservoir would destroy a 25-mile stretch of the river along with forests and lakes of the State Forest Preserve in the heart of the Adirondack Park.

In a brief statement after the vote, Schaefer said there had been "a mandate" by the people to preserve the wild country and he lauded the legislature's action.

Schaefer had urged adoption of the measure to Assembly Speaker Perry R. Duryea Jr. as well as other legislators.

Assemblyman Clark C. Wemple, R-Schenectady, maintained other water supply sources should be sought by New York City.

* * *

Among possibilities, he mentioned extraction of river water from the lower Hudson, desalization of sea water and the use of subsurface supplies.

The state water resources commission had endorsed the dam, saying surface water is the best source for New York City and that the Gooley dam project had the greatest potential storage.

There was virtually no opposition at hearings on the legislation when Schaefer and others noted the Hamlet of New comb would be all but wiped out.

* * *

Sen. Walter B. Langley, R-Albany and Schoharie Counties, was co-sponsor of the bill, which was introduced by Republicans

Sen. Bernard C. Smith, Northport, and Assemblyman Clarence Lane, Windham, conservation committee chairmen.

the recycling of water by large municipalities, and cleaning it, or moving it up river to mix with other fresh waters on the way down, nor have we fully investigated the stores of underground water. Every year the likelihood of getting fresh water from the limitless waters of the ocean becomes more certain because of technological break-throughs in desalinization. Progress in the atmospheric sciences also promises aid in the future.

The proposition that we should continue to solve the water problems of the late twentieth century with nineteenth-century methods, destroying our favored wilderness and pastoral valleys in the process, is ridiculous!

Can the state involve itself in any greater conservation program than one that would assure the permanent preservation of the Upper Hudson River? In the process of carrying out such an objective, can we not make this region even more usable to our people and at the same time coordinate a policy with the private landowners in the region?

The people of New York State want more, not less, protection for their world-famous Adirondack Park. They want more, not fewer rivers in which to canoe, glacial lakes in which to fish, forests in which to hunt, and wildlife to see and enjoy. For them, this is a priceless and irreplaceable inheritance dreamed of by statesmen nearly a century ago and gradually built into a reality.

This is a time for decision on the Upper Hudson—a time for engineers and conservationists to embark on programs of research and water management of sufficient wisdom and magnitude to solve such problems as confront us!

It is fundamental that we preserve the Upper Hudson so that posterity, too, can know the beauty and the wonder of this wild, untamed river, which quickens the pulse and so well symbolizes the dynamic powers of nature that have shaped the world we live in.

5

National Concern
for the Adirondacks

Trail at the Flowed Lands. "Paul *(taking the photo)*, I *(left)*, and Ed *(right)* started off on one of the best trips I have ever had"—Howard Zahniser, Diary, Avalanche Pass, 1946.

One bitter cold day in February 1930, I found myself climbing the precipitous slopes of the Helderberg Mountains, which are located about twenty miles west of Albany, New York. My objective was the Copperhead Cave, a historic hideaway for Tory spies during the Revolution. From its entrance, high in the limestone cliffs a thousand feet above the valley, the city could be seen across the undulating plains. A great chunk of the cliff above the cave had fallen across the entrance, protecting the interior of the cave from the elements. This cave and these mountains had started Verplanck Colvin on his lifelong Adirondack odyssey when he wrote about them for *Harper's New Monthly Magazine* in 1869. This same cave, in turn, was to profoundly affect my life.

Reaching the cave, I was startled to see numerous slender columns of ice—stalagmites—rising from the floor to a height of about five feet. They varied in diameter from bottom to top and were so fragile that a good wind would have demolished them. After photographing them, I hurried home with my discovery. When the photographs were developed several days later, it occurred to me that perhaps a national magazine would be interested. I had a copy of *Nature Magazine* in my den with my first Adirondack books, so I sent the photo to the publisher's office in Washington. In a few days, I had received an acknowledgment and an offer for payment. I was, of course, thrilled.

Less than two years later, we found ourselves faced with an issue that would, if successful, doom wilderness in the Adirondacks. It was the "closed cabin" amendment to the New York State Constitution, and it would have permitted cabin colonies to be built anywhere in the forest preserve by any public authority with legislative approval. The New York State Legislature had twice approved the proposal, and it was to be settled by the people in the election of 1932. It occurred to me that if a national magazine would be interested in a cave in some almost unknown mountains, they might be concerned with the possible loss of the Adirondack wilderness. *Nature* magazine was interested, and they requested an article as soon as possible. They published my hastily written essay "Defend the Wilderness" in August 1932 and capped it with an editorial fine enough to be quoted by historian Philip Terrie in his centennial book *Forever Wild*, which was published in 1985 by Temple University Press.

Twelve years later, we were faced with a proposal by foresters to lumber the forest preserve, and I prepared "Adirondack Forests in Peril." This time *National Parks* magazine published it, and by focusing attention on foresters nationally the proposal was killed.

Two years later, a proposal surfaced that would inundate the finest river and lake country in the Moose River region. John Apperson and I had been requested to present a documentary film and a slide show to the Eleventh National Wildlife Conference in New York City. This we did, and immediately after the presentation, Howard Zahniser, Executive Secretary of the Wilderness Society, and Carl Gutermuth of the Wildlife Management Institute came up and offered us editorial and financial assistance in our battle to save that wilderness. When I mentioned the fact that I had joined hands with Bob Marshall in the Adirondacks in 1932, Zahniser became intensely interested.

Three major essays followed during the next fifteen years. Each focused national attention on the Adirondacks. Most importantly, Zahniser involved himself and the Wilderness Society to an amazing extent in the next eighteen years. He became our national representative, attended public hearings by state agencies, and testified eloquently in our behalf.

Our meeting in New York City was to become as fateful to wilderness in New York as was my meeting with Bob Marshall atop Mount Marcy fourteen years earlier.

Howard Zahniser was inspired by New York's "forever wild" constitutional covenant, and he was determined to get the National Wilderness Preservation Act approved by the United States Congress that would include the essence of New York's constitutional "forever wild" clause. This was accomplished in 1964, and as of today more than ninety million acres are protected by that national covenant.

Defend the Wilderness

The lands of the state, now owned or hereafter acquired, constituting the forest preserve as now fixed by law, shall forever be kept as wild forest lands. They shall not be leased, sold, or exchanged, or taken by any corporation, public or private, nor shall the timber thereon be sold, removed or destroyed.

Thus reads Section 7 of Article VII of the New York State Constitution. Adopted unanimously by the Constitutional Convention in 1894, this "Gibraltar of Forestry" has withstood the test of time and weathered repeated attacks of commercial interests. Today it is the guardian of more than two million acres of state land in the Adirondack Park, a mountain region of unexcelled charm and rugged beauty except where man had earlier wantonly and ruthlessly destroyed portions of it.

Inspired by wholesale timber and land thefts in the Adirondacks, the article became effective immediately upon ratification by the people in 1895. The damage done by the despoilers had assumed such tremendous proportions, however, that the magnificent virgin forests of northern New York were sadly depleted. Great private holdings continued to be the scene of lumbering operations. Fire followed many of the cuttings and from time to time great areas of the protected forests went up in smoke. Acquisition of land by the state has hardly kept pace with the steady inroads of civilization and its consequent development. The constitutional covenant has served its ideal admirably, and yet its real worth is just beginning to be recognized by conservationists generally, many of whom until recently have held that its terms were too strict for

Reprinted from *Nature* magazine, August 1932.

Silver Lakes Wilderness. Shall we bequeath the youth of tomorrow a land stripped of wilderness . . . or shall they be heir to a region magnificent with hulking mountains, long reaches of forest giants, quiet woodland trails with gemlike lakes and tumbling rivers beyond? Photograph courtesy of NYS Department of Environmental Conservation.

practical purposes. Its existence is the sole reason for the remaining glory of these "oldest mountains on earth."

At the polls this November [of 1932] the voters of New York will either reaffirm their belief in the forest protection instrument now an integral part of their constitution, or they will adopt the so-called Porter-Brereton Recreation Amendment, which is in fact a nullification of the existing law. Briefly it is an "all-tame forest versus part-wild forest" decision they will make. The issue has assumed stupendous proportions, and conservationists the nation over have expressed deep concern as to the outcome. Unquestionably the future park policy of other major mountain ranges will be directly affected by the decision.

A careful study of the issue as a whole reveals many interesting facts, foremost among them being that while the conditions which actuated Section 7 of Article VII have themselves been controlled, far greater problems of forest preserve exploitation must be met than those which existed in 1894. Scenic regions free from commercialization have become increasingly scarce until today it takes but little vision to see that unless conservationists fight hard in every quarter, the wilderness is doomed!

According to its author, a chief reason for the amendment is a desire to see the forest preserve "open to the public for recreational uses and not frozen in as a jungle for wild animals." Such a statement is indefensible in the light of facts.

More than half of the entire seven thousand square miles within the Adirondack Park is still privately owned and subject to development of any description. Thousands of acres in the heart of this so-called "jungle" are recovering from exploitation. They are a tragic remainder of the wanton destruction which prompted constitutional protection. Many hotels dot the entire area, some of them little removed from the High Peaks region. A network of roads enables one to visit many parts of the park without having to spend a single night out-of-doors. There are thriving towns and villages with one-way streets, theatres, underpasses, and most of the other adjuncts of our larger cities. Private interests control hundreds of thousands of acres of wooded areas in the heart of the park. Great lumbering operations are at this moment stripping the upper watershed of the Hudson River of its all-important trees. On the shore of what is quite commonly called "the most beautiful lake in America," a five-story hotel has been built.

It is proposed to build "recreation buildings" that would be operated for gain on public lands. With the nature of these buildings not being specified, it seems inevitable that soft-drink stands, dance halls, and other undesirable structures would in time become located in the best of our scenic regions. Trees could be cut for all of these purposes. The amendment also stipulates that existing public roads may be improved. Almost any sort of a trail could legally be termed a road, and promiscuous road building would ultimately result. Under the present law, the people decide by direct vote just where highways can be constructed.

This voice in the development of the park would be lost if the amendment is successful. Also, unless specifically indicated by each legislative act, the conservation department would have no jurisdiction over the various projects authorized by the amendment. The harm possible because of such wide diversification of control is almost incalculable.

Every type of recreation may now be found within the park. Nearly half a million people used the state campsites last year. These sites, in all parts of the park, are in the charge of rangers and have many modern conveniences. Hundred of thousands use the foot trails, and the open shelter system is used more extensively than ever before. Other hundreds of thousands of people enjoyed the various amusements operated by private enterprise.

Need more be said about this "jungle for wild animals"?

Conservationists should remember that the constitutional limitation of development which affects the Adirondack Park does not apply to the state production forests outside its boundaries, nor to the large number of lesser state parks where all kinds of amusement buildings are not only permitted but encouraged by the government. It should also be remembered that this is our last frontier, and even with the aid of Section 7 of Article VII it will be a tremendous undertaking to preserve the natural woodland character, the value of which is just beginning to become recognized.

What of the youth of tomorrow? Shall we bequeath to them a land stripped of wilderness? Or shall they be heir to a region magnificent with hulking mountains, long reaches of forest giants, quiet woodland trails with the gemlike lakes and tumbling rivers beyond? And shall we preserve for them a place, where in the shadow of the hills they can pitch their tents, and there by the side of his glowing campfire, exult in knowing that strange new experience of being in country untamed?

It is not enough that all of our many conservation organizations have taken steps to defeat this new attempt to exploit our mountains. It is not enough that the governor, his lieutenant, and such public-spirited men have declared themselves opposed to the proposal. Individual, self-actuating effort is the only antidote for the mass indifference that exists on this question.

We must remember that defeat means disaster!

Adirondack Forests in Peril

The scene was the state capitol, Albany, New York. The time was September 8, 1894. A constitutional convention was in session, with the usual solemnity and dignity which ordinarily may be found on such an occasion. Statemanship and political intrigue in such extremes as probably may be found only in such a state as New York, found voice among the people's representatives.

Colonel David McClure, chairman of the Committee on Forest Preservation addressed the convention and said in part:

> We stood here on the eighth of May feeling that the people of this state were convinced that they were living under a good constitution and did not need any actual, positive, or sweeping change. And yet, one great matter affecting not the success, temporary or permanent, of any party, nor affecting any corporations or individuals in their own selfish interests, but vitally affecting the people of the state and their great necessity, stood crying for relief at the hands of this convention. The hills, rock-ribbed and ancient as the sun, the venerable woods, rivers that move in majesty, and complaining brooks that make the meadows green, these for years have been neglected by the people of the state and the great men out of state.

David McClure was speaking of the Adirondack Mountains in northern New York, with their two thousand peaks, twenty-seven hundred lakes and ponds, dozens of rivers and a wilderness unsurpassed in beauty by any in America.

Swift destruction was laying waste to these forests which pro-

Reprinted by permission from *National Parks* magazine, July–September, 1945. Copyright © 1945 by National Parks and Conservation Association.

Rushing water on the East Branch of the Sacandaga. "The hills, rock-ribbed and ancient as the sun, the venerable woods, rivers that move in majesty, and complaining brooks that make the meadows green, these for years have been neglected by the people . . . and the great men of the state"—David McClure, Constitutional Convention, 1894. Photograph by Noel Riedinger-Johnson.

tected the upper watershed of the Hudson, the Saranac, the Black, the Moose, the Beaver, the Ausable, and other important rivers. Eighty thousand acres of this primeval woods were being cut annually. The easily accessible bottomland forests were rapidly disappearing, and the mountain slopes with their irreplaceable evergreens were threatened with the same devastation.

McClure spoke eloquently of these dangers and then presented the following proposal which was unanimously adopted by the convention a few days later: "The lands of the state, now owned or hereafter acquired, constituting the forest preserve as now fixed by law, shall be forever kept as wild forest lands."

In November the people of the state approved this in constitutional referendum, and it became the famous "forever wild" legislation, which went into effect in 1895.

The theory was that the Adirondack forests should remain inviolate for their watershed values and for the health and recreational uses of the people. The enormous population of the state made it necessary that these primary values be given such consideration, as against lumbering and the ever-present threat of forest fires that quickly and often permanently destroy such values.

As would be expected, this constitutional provision has been under constant attack by commercial interests for a half century. It has successfully weathered the most violent storms and remains today substantially unchanged from its original form. As recently as 1938, another constitutional convention reaffirmed this historic forest protective policy. The question of lumbering the Adirondack Forest Preserve was then thoroughly debated. More than fifty organizations, including all the important statewide conservation and sportsmen's groups, supported this provision and again the people approved it at the polls.

Once more, however, the advocates of lumbering are marshaling their forces with the stated intent of breaking down this protection of forest preserve lands in both the Adirondack and the Catskill state parks.

In the April 1944 issue of the *New York Forester*, the publication of the New York Section of the Society of American Foresters, there appears an account of its annual meeting. The highlight of the session was the approval of the following resolution, against the advice of several of the older members of the section: "that the New York Section of the Society of American Foresters hereby goes on record as favoring a constitutional amendment to Article XIV, Section 1, of the state constitution, to permit scientific management of the forest preserve; and that it instruct its officers to take appropriate action to bring this resolution to the attention of the appropriate members of the state government."

Subsequently the new chairman of the New York Section made an address over the radio urging that the forest preserve be lumbered. This was given wide publicity throughout the state press. Other members and some state officals have been advocating such action. Adirondack lumbermen and millowners, watching the privately owned timberlands disappear, have been discussing the question openly and in the press. Some influential papers approve such proposed action.

The Adirondack Mountain Club, recognizing the danger, has not only reiterated its traditional position on the question, but has caused a brief to be written explaining its opposition to such lumbering. The Forest Preserve Association of New York State has been in the field actively countering the new threat with its film entitled *Scientific Forestry* which shows current lumber operations on private lands, forest fire devastation, soil erosion, and related subjects.

The problem may be summed up briefly as follows:

The Adirondack Park consists of about 5,500,000 acres, Of this, the state owns 2,172,000 acres with the balance privately owned and subject to virtually any kind of exploitation. More than a million acres are held by lumber companies, with much of such land being lumbered excessively. The remaining land is in private estates, both large and small, mining corporations, municipalities and thousands of small farms, tourist places, and similar holdings.

Most of the state forest preserve has been lumbered at least once. Much of it has burned. More than 300,000 acres lie above 2,500 feet, the elevation where New York foresters generally agree that no lumbering should take place because of thin soil, high watershed values and possible complete destruction of forest and soil by burning and erosion.

By process of deduction, it becomes clear that the forests which are the target of those who would lumber the preserve are the last remaining stands of virgin pines in the Oswegatchie River headwaters and the spruce and hemlock in the Raquette Lake region in the northwestern and central parts of the park. Other areas in danger would be those lands that have been in state ownership many decades and where the forest has recovered from the original lumber operation.

The fact that these lands in their natural state as required by the constitution are best suited for watershed protection and increasing recreational needs is of little or no consequence to the advocates of lumbering. On many hundred thousand acres of such land, the original cutting removed only the softwood trees of the mixed virgin forest. The softwood stumps have rotted away, and to all appearance the land is virgin hardwood country in which the only evidence of the ax is to be found in occasional ruins of lumber camps, tote roads, or log dams on rivers and streams.

The so-called managed forestry program which people have expected would be carried out on private lands in these mountains has been, with few exceptions, abandoned. According to an official state report in 1944, the white pine stand on private lands is being cut so excessively that by 1949, at the present rate of cutting, this resource will have been completely liquidated commercially in the Adirondacks. This was once the most prolific pine region in the East. For the first time in decades, the hardwoods are being cut by many operators with modern machinery, roads, and transportation making movement of this material economically possible.

Forest preserve lands are scattered in several hundred parcels throughout the length and breadth of the park. As a result, private lumber operations intermix with state holdings in many places, thereby endangering protected land. Lumber operations which have clean-cut the forest along scenic highways are not uncommon. It may thus be concluded that the lumbermen, in the absence of a state law regulating the cutting of small trees, are taking not only the accrued interest from their holdings, but in many cases are withdrawing the principal account, leaving the Adirondacks stripped.

An important argument conservationists use against lumbering the forest preserve is the peculiar nature of the soil. Vegetable in composition, it has a thickness of but a few inches to scarcely more than a foot on the mountain slopes. This thin layer of soil or humus is underlain with extremely hard rocks such as gneiss, intrusive granite, and gabbro. A forest fire burns this soil as completely as the timber at times, and what it does not burn it lays open to the forces of erosion which soon wash the mountain slope clean of soil. Examples of this type of devastation are to be found in virtually all parts of the Adirondacks, with dozens of major peaks completely or substantially devastated. It is hardly necessary to add that as a result of such destruction, watershed values have been seriously impaired, and streams, located where they could be of inestimable value to the state for their recreational uses, flood and dry up intermittently. The existing law makes further destruction of watershed and recreation values impossible except in the case of fire, which can usually be easily controlled where not fed by lumbering debris.

An excellent picture of existing values in the Adirondacks is found in a paragraph from a conservation department bulletin entitled, "Registered Guides of New York State" dated 1943:

> The conservation department has jurisdiction over the forest preserve which now includes nearly two million acres and is immediately accessible to approximately ten million people. Thus, on account of both its size and the large number of people living within a short distance of it, it is probably the most important public preserve in the United States, from the standpoint of recreation. One of the fundamental purposes for which the forest preserve was established was to make a great vacation ground for the citizens of the state. That this object is being realized is indicated by the fact that in the forest preserve region more money has already been invested in hotels and other properties for caring for vacationists, more people are employed in this work and more money is paid them in wages, than in the lumber business itself, which was once the chief industry of the country.

The state maintains a system of public campsites that annually attract three-quarters of a million people. These campsites are located in outstanding scenic areas, along rivers and on lake shores. Firewood and sanitary facilities are provided free, with the camper otherwise being on his own. In addition there are to be found open lean-tos in the high peaks and other regions. Trails thread the interior, and although roads have been limited generally to the arteries of access, all of the several thousand lakes, ponds, and mountains are within a day's walking distance from the highways. Hunters and fishermen by the thousand are attracted to the more remote interior in season. Winter sports have come into their own, and before the war, snow trains were run whenever the weather favored such sports.

Perhaps the best judicial decision rendered by the courts as to the meaning and intent of the constitutional forest law was made by Justice Harold Hinman in 1930:

> Giving to the phrase "forever kept as wild forest lands" the significance which the terms "wild forest" bears, we must conclude that the idea intended was a health resort and playground designed somewhat after the widely accepted pattern of our world-famous wilderness national parks. We must preserve its trees, its rocks, its streams, in their wild state. It was to be a great resort for the free use of the people in which nature is given free reign. Its uses for

health and pleasure must not be inconsistent with its preservation as forest lands in a wild state. It must always retain the character of a wilderness. Hunting, fishing, tramping, mountain climbing, snowshoeing, skiing, or skating find an ideal setting in nature's wilderness. It is essentially a quiet and healthful retreat from the turmoils and artificialities of a busy urban life.

Thus is the issue drawn.

Shall the Adirondack Park lose its unique wild-forest character by lumbering which will yield questionable renumeration to the state? Shall one of the last areas in eastern America to retain virgin forest, now of great educational value, be stripped for an inconsequential postponement of the day of more acute timber shortage in New York State? Would not such logging postpone the day when the state must vigorously pursue reforestation of its more than five million acres of barren, submarginal land? What can the lumbermen or foresters offer the public in the Adirondacks as good examples of forest management that they would put into effect on forest preserve lands? Is not this history largely one of bankruptcy of forest resources and the devastation of such lands?

Careful study of the mountains themselves leads to the logical answer that the main purpose of the Adirondack forest preserve is to protect the sources of our major rivers and streams and to provide a recreation land for the millions of our citizens.

The only certain way that these values can be retained is to keep intact the most potent of all conservation laws, Article XIV, Section 1, of the New York State Constitution, which declares that "the lands of the state . . . shall be forever kept as wild forest lands."

Roaring Brook Falls, Keene Valley. Natural beauty in abundance is the underlying feature of the region.

The Adirondack

PATTERN OF A BATTLE FOR WOODS AND WATERS

Carved by the glaciers or the icebergs of the drift period from the most ancient granite of the world's formation, washed and eroded by the storms of a thousand centuries, the Adirondack ranges rise in dark and gloomy billows, stretching from the hills which skirt the Mohawk away northward to the shores of the river from which this most ancient rock takes the term Laurentian. Elsewhere are mountains more stupendous, more icy and more dreary, but none look down upon a grander landscape, in rich autumn time, more brightly gemmed or jeweled with innumerable lakes, or crystal pools, or wild with savage chasms, or of primeval forest stretched over range upon range to the far horizon, where the sea of mountains fades into a dim, vaporous uncertainty. A region of mystery, over which none can gaze without a strange thrill of interest and of a wonder at what may be hidden in that vast area of forest, covering all things with its deep repose.

Thus did Verplanck Colvin, superintendent of the Adirondack Topographical Survey, write in 1879, after fourteen years exploration of the region. His was the youthful voice that cried out for the preservation of the Adirondack wilderness in the dignified chambers of the legislature, before historical and art societies, before the powerful businessmen's group, the New York Board of Trade and Transportation, and to individuals everywhere, in city and hamlet and around the flickering light of his campfire in the land he loved so well. Thus he helped in the battle that culminated in the pas-

Reprinted, with changes, from the *Living Wilderness*, March 1946, by permission of The Wilderness Society.

sage of that "best loved and most hated" of all conservation measures —Article VII, Section 7, of the 1894 state constitution, the famous "forever wild" clause.

For a half century now, this instrument has inspired men to devote their lives and their fortunes to its defense. It has likewise been the target for ceaseless attacks by commercial interests, but it remains substantially unchanged today.

The Adirondack Park with its 8,555 square miles is the largest public preserve in the United States and is immediately accessible to more than ten million people. [In 1986 over fifty-five million people live within a day's drive of the park.] Only about half of the park is state-owned and thus protected by the constitution. The balance is privately owned and subject to virtually any kind of exploitation—from vast lumbering operations to open-pit mining, from the Swiss-like farms of the mountaineers to the large hotels with the ultimate in tourist cuisine.

The vast primeval wilderness described by Colvin has long since followed the passenger pigeon into the realm from which there is no return. Man and fire have devastated thousands of acres of irreplaceable forests at the sources of our most important rivers and streams. Commercial interests have destroyed lake and river regions of matchless beauty, and are threatening others. The critical demands of war have wreaked havoc on private lands within the park. And still other interests, including advocates of commercialized recreation on state lands, are gathering their forces for an assault upon this region which if not checked will permanently destroy much of the unique wild-forest charm of the Adirondacks.

Thus, when one views the Adirondack problem in proper perspective he must remember that this land of two thousand mountain peaks, nearly twenty-eight hundred lakes and ponds, fifty rivers, and innumerable streams is already delicately balanced between the best kind of mountain protection by the state and the worst kind of exploitation by some private interests.

Let us briefly examine some of the threats to these mountains with the hope that by clear recognition of the pending attacks we can properly evaluate the dangers at hand and rise to the occasion required.

Commericalized recreation is one of these hazards. For many years, efforts have been made to put the state into the permanent camp and amusement business in the Adirondacks. An attack in this direction has again been made by means of the so-called Young-Reoux "Recreation" Amendment to permit "building and maintaining in the forest preserve permanent enclosed buildings of use to the public for healthful recreation." Till now one of the safeguards of the forest preserve has been a ruling of the courts that closed buildings on state forest preserve lands are not permitted, except for administrative personnel such as forest rangers and fire observers. And the Adirondack Mountain Club is now spearheading a fight against the proposed amendment that would remove this safeguard. As the club points out in a pamphlet just released:

> The backers of this proposal plan to substitute for free outdoor enjoyment in Nature's wilderness, vacation resort developments financed by the state. This amendment, it is claimed, "will open the forest preserve to the public." On the contrary it will actually keep most of the public out of the hundreds of beauty spots which are now free to all comers, by locating "permanent enclosed buildings" in the choicest areas. Other locations are more suitable and appropriate for the establishment of the type of facilities apparently intended in this amendment. We are not opposed to any kind of recreation, but it seems clear that the type of recreation should be suited to the surroundings.

More than half the area of the park, the club emphasizes, is privately owned. "Permanent enclosed buildings" do not exist in large number. As many more as are needed can be built and operated, and thus any desired recreation programs can be carried out on the private lands. Furthermore, the club says:

> Within the limitations of Article XIV, the Conservation Department has developed, and now successfully maintains, a recreational program in the preserve, consistent with its true character. This included 574 miles of foot trails, 111 miles of ski trails, 163 open lean-tos, and 29 public campsites under the best sanitary regulations. The postwar program provides for a 50 percent increase in the number of campsites. The entire area of the preserve is open to hunting and fishing in season. Hundreds of miles of streams and more than a thousand lakes and ponds are available for the free use of boaters, canoeists, and swimmers. Prior to the war more than three-quarters of a million people annually enjoyed the free use of the campsites, in addition to which hundreds of thousands hiked the trails, camped in lean-tos, climbed the mountains, swam the lakes, canoed in both lakes and streams, hunted in the forests, and fished in the waters of these unique woodland parks. And except for the nominal hunting and fishing license fees, the proceeds of which are used exclusively for law enforcement and the propagation of fish and game, it was and still is all free.

The great attraction of these mountains to the tourist and sports-
man, to say nothing of the hiker or the mountaineering people, is the
large area of wild forest land owned by the state. Natural beauty in
an abundant quantity is the underlying feature of the region. There
seems, therefore, little question but that the people, while approving
such camps or cottages in the scores of state parks not in the forest preserve, will—if the issue is made clear—continue to support policies
that accentuate the high values of land with wild-forest character in the
forest preserve itself. But it is an issue that must be made clear, and perhaps there may yet be a battle to win on this front as well as on many
others.

Impending tragedy in the Moose River region is in the form of
dam proposals—another hazard in preservation of the forest preserve.

Situated in the southwestern part of the Adirondack Park, this
Moose River region comprises nearly a thousand square miles of heavily forested mountain country with gemlike lakes and innumerable rivers and streams. It is considered by many to be the finest remnant of
primitive woodland left in eastern America, and it is the largest area in
New York not yet bisected by a highway.

Near the heart of this extensive region are the famous Moose
River Plains, comprising about seven hundred acres. Much of the area
is open grassland, but it has peninsulas of trees reaching out from the
heavy surrounding forest. Also there are what may be called oases of
evergreens, which thickly cover portions of the plains that drop thirty
or more feet below the general level of the land. Adjacent to the plains,
and in the Beaver Lake and Indian River regions nearby, are magnificent stands of the original pine and spruce forests, with pines more than
five feet in diameter and nearly 150 feet or more tall.

This is the most extensive winter-yarding ground for white-tailed
deer in the state. Less common species of wildlife such as the otter, the
fisher, and the marten are also found here. Other animals and birds,
both large and small, probably maintain as primitive a natural balance
here as in any place in the East, and certainly the profusion of wildlife
surpasses that of any other region in New York State.

The rivers and streams—born on heavily forested mountain slopes
and in lush, green beds of sphagnum moss that carpet the ledge and
lowland—are cold and pure, and like the small glacial lakes of the region, they abound with trout.

Trails reach the interior from four points of the compass. Even
now it is an important Adirondack recreation land, and probably it is
New York State's best potential for the hiker and camper who has a
yen for the wilderness.

This is the land of which more than eight thousand acres would be inundated by the proposed Higley Mountain and Panther Mountain reservoirs on the South Branch of the Moose River. Designed for hydroelectric and stream regulation purposes (for which there is questionable need), they would eliminate the multiple values of the entire area by destroying its heart, with the food and shelter for wildlife, and by bisecting the area with roads.

The many miles of river with deep, dark pools, and riffles and rapids, flanked with the spires of the evergreen forests, would become but a memory. The open plains, over which hang the tranquillity of ageless things, would be irrevocably lost for all time. The forests, of inspiring beauty—including one of the last stands of original forest in all the East—would be laid low. And who can recall the primitive beauty of a glacial pond, set like a gem in this lush, green land?

What greater tragedy could there be than to destroy such irreplaceable landscapes and waterscapes, so rich with wildlife, so abundant with the requirements of posterity?

Shall the forest preserve be lumbered? This is the issue over which the original battle of the Adirondacks was fought, and for some time conservationists have felt that the forest preserve was secure against lumbering, under any name, including scientific forest management. After smoldering for years, however, an organized attempt broke out last year to line up forces in behalf of the lumbermen, who in some cases have so mismanaged their own lands as to leave them useless for the production of timber.

Stands of white pine privately owned in the Adirondacks are being cut so thoroughly and extensively that this resource is being liquidated completely in this the most prolific pine region in the East. On many lumber jobs, there is no such thing as selective cutting. Much of this prime land is being permanently lost as such, since after clear-cutting these lands commonly reproduce hardwoods instead of the original species.

Recently, for the first time in decades, there has also been substantial hardwood cutting in this region on private lands. The portable mill, the tractor, and the road-building bulldozer have made heretofore inaccessible stands of timber available.

It is well known that the last remaining stands of virgin white pine, hemlock, and spruce, totaling probably 100,000 acres, would be the first timber to fall under the ax if an amendment were passed legalizing forest management. Other substantial areas of recovered forests would soon follow.

According to a recent state report, more than a million acres or nearly half of the forest preserve has insufficient saleable timber on it to justify cutting. Some of it has been burned beyond hope of recovery for centuries, and the Adirondack Mountain Club has, in fact, pointed out that "the most eloquent and compelling arguments against lumbering the forest preserve are to be found in the burned, ravaged, and devastated mountains themselves."

Yet lumbering interests are reaching for the trees still tempting to them, and the use of these forests for the protection of water sources, as well as for recreation, is another value of the Adirondacks that conservationists have constantly to defend.

Mining and pollution are further threats. Early in 1945 a constitutional amendment was introduced in the New York Legislature that proposed to permit the mining of "gold, silver, ores or minerals" on forest preserve lands. This measure, although opposed by virtually all of the scores of sportsmen's, mountain, and hiking clubs, including the powerful New York State Conservation Council representing a half-million sportsmen, passed both houses of the legislature almost unanimously. Before it can be adopted it must be passed by the succeeding legislature (the one beginning January 1, 1947) for second approval, and it must subsequently be approved by a referendum of the people. Conservationists will fight it at every step.

Much of the mining in the Adirondacks is open-pit mining, which not only destroys land and forest but often pollutes streams. The pollution is inorganic and destroys aquatic life by the accumulation of silt on the beds of streams and lakes. Furthermore, it makes the water unfit for swimming or drinking, for though it is safe for such use, human nature rebels at the thought of vacationing along waters that instead of being crystal clear are dark and muddy, with rocks covered by a slippery, claylike substance and pools silted in.

A classic example of the devastation caused by mining may be found at Sanford Lake, near the source of the Hudson River, in the heart of the Adirondacks. Here the National Lead Company is obtaining iron, titanium, and vanadium in extensive quantities. The operation uses the entire volume of the river at times. The water is dumped by sluicing directly into Sanford Lake, once a crystal-clear lake seven miles long in the famed Tahawus valley. More than half a million tons of solids are being dumped each year into this lake, gradually filling it solid with refuse and polluting the Hudson River for miles below. Fish and aquatic life in the lake have already been largely destroyed. According to pollution scientists, it is only a matter of time until the rivers in the Adirondacks will be devoid of such life as now exists, unless the destruction is stopped. (Conservationists are watching with interest an experiment by the company in constructing a settling basin which may prevent some of the pollution).

This type of operation is on private land, in a valley that contains both private and state holdings. Obviously most of the value of the state holdings are destroyed by such private operations, which affect camping, fishing, and swimming for many miles below the scene of the actual mining operation.

As for the mining amendment, geologists say there is virtually no gold or silver in these mountains, but minerals and ores are common. Conservationists realize that if the amendment is passed, and a deposit of iron ore, titanium, graphite, or garnet is found in a remote area, its development could bring highways, buildings, and all other adjuncts of modern civilization into the wildest part of the region, without further constitutional amendment.

It is very evident that a hard fight will be required to defeat the mining amendment and an even more difficult effort required to prevent the pollution of our rivers by operations on private lands.

Lake George possesses a natural beauty unsurpassed by any lake in America, yet it has been made into a millpond! More than thirty miles long, its crystal waters dotted with nearly two hundred islands, it lies between spectacular mountains at the southeastern gateway to the Adirondacks. For three hundred years it has inspired the traveler, from its discoverer, the Jesuit Father Isaac Jogues, to the throngs which now converge on it at every opportunity.

At the northern end of the lake is a natural stone dam which had regulated the water level from time immemorial, permitting and maintaining the formation of soil and luxuriant vegetation close to the water's edge along the shores—until some years ago, when parts of this natural stone dam were blasted out to afford more waterhead for use of a mill at the outlet falls. A dam was then built higher than the original dam, making possible water levels both higher and lower than those naturally regulated. As a consequence, serious destruction of soil, tree, and plant growth has occurred. Some of the small islands which once supported trees have disappeared entirely, except for dangerous rock shoals that serve as fitting monuments to the selfishness of man in destroying such masterpieces of nature.

Most of the islands and many miles of the shoreline are forest preserve land, and according to the constitution must "be forever kept as wild forest lands." Yet, incredible as it may seem, it has actually taken conservationists more than thirty years of intense effort to bring this issue to a head. Only last summer did the case reach the courts, where the state and some shore owners charged the mill owner with trespass and damage. At this point the case now rests, for the decision of the court will be based upon evidence already presented.

Roads in the forest preserve are already adequate, yet more are constantly proposed. Generally speaking, it may be said that the Adirondacks have a sufficient network of roads to make the woods readily accessible. The best proof of this is the fact that it is now possible to visit by foot virtually any part of the entire park (except the Moose River region) and return to a highway within a day. Yet there is always pressure for roads and more roads. The motivation for many road-building attempts in these mountains is the private interests of those who desire accessibility to their lands for economic advantage. There is also the interest of motorists who want to drive fast, by the shortest possible route, and who do not understand that they can enjoy such driving just as much without cutting up wild areas into a network of roads and thus spoiling other people's pleasure.

Adirondack conservationists fearing destructive highway programs are now most closely watching the developments in connection with a "super-road" project being advocated by Senator James Mead of New York. It has been rumored that this might bisect the Adirondacks through the famous Oswegatchie forest, yet the Senator, it is reported by his office, has no specific route in mind as yet. Most recently the project has been suggested as a memorial to the late President Roosevelt, and conservationists know that to be an appropriate memorial to him the road should not damage wilderness areas. Those who knew Mr. Roosevelt point out that a destruction of wild areas would be the last kind of memorial he would want, for in both his public life and his private activities he put much emphasis on natural beauty and on the preservation of the Adirondack wild forest region. Conservationists are convinced that, in the main, road building in these northern mountains should be confined to the improvement of existing arteries of access.

Invasion of the woods by airplane and jeep is another emerging problem now getting attention in New York. Invasion of wild places by the airplane and the versatile jeep, it is realized, will in themselves exert extraordinary pressure on the woods even without further roads. The forest preserve is honeycombed with old abandoned lumber roads that may be traversed by the jeep unless restrictions are placed on such use by the state conservation department. In like manner, many of the fifteen hundred lakes and ponds will lose their solitude and chief attraction unless landing on such waters is prohibited by the same state department, which is now considering such action.

At various intervals during the last half century, there have been funds for buying land for the forest preserve made available through bond issues which the people approved by referendum. The state was thereby in the position to take advantage of opportunities to round out its scattered holdings whenever land became available. For several years, however, these funds have been exhausted, and with the exception of an occasional grant by the legislature for a specific purpose, there has been no money available for land purchase. And this situation has existed at a time when New York State has had a large surplus in its treasury.

Certain powers-that-be have made it clear that unless such concessions as closed camps and road building on state land are made, they will block any proposed bond issue for Adirondack use. Such a short-sighted policy clearly runs counter to the public interest, and an effort should begin at once to make available funds to increase state holdings in line with the vastly increased recreational use of the region.

Concluding this overview of problems, we should point out that, in addition to the larger issues, we have with us constantly many minor projects which tend to whittle away the wild-forest character of the forest preserve. Some of these are sponsored by well-meaning public officials, others are studied attempts to achieve an unlawful end by apparently harmless means. We must be alive to such dangers and understand that a combination of minor encroachments can add up to a serious loss to the woods.

The Adirondack problem is thus similar in general pattern to problems affecting the entire park system of the nation, yet it has important elements that differ from those found in many other regions. Most important of these is probably the tremendous population living close to these mountains. More than ten million people live within a three hundred mile radius of the park boundaries. This accentuates pressure on the region. At the same time, it could conceivably be the factor that would make possible a secure protection of the forest preserve based on the wise use of its mountains for health and pleasure. Preservation of the all-important constitutional provision is, as a matter of historical record, largely due to the votes of the large cities, including New York, in turning down attempts to commercialize the woods. Some of the most effective supporters of wild-forest lands come from the engineering and research laboratories of Schenectady, the parkways

South Branch of the Moose River. It was nothing new that we were alarmed lest the things we treasured so greatly should be lost in the thoughtless, heedless rush of modern, mechanized civilization.

of Albany, and the canyons of New York City. Each new attack on the Adirondacks finds these people working with men and women of sister cities and with the big, quiet men of mountain village and hamlet. Here are Virginians and Texans and Californians, as well as native sons and daughters, who believe in sustaining this obviously most beneficial law that has removed the Adirondack woods and waters from the grasp of politicians and has put them into the hands of the people.

Typical of how New York State is united on such preservation is the present all-out battle for the preservation of the Moose River region. As late as September 1945, not a single outdoor club in the state was fighting the proposed devastation since the public hearings on the project had been held during the darkest days of the war in a small upstate village. Several of us, in September 1945, made a study of the problem and reached the conclusion that one of the irreplaceable regions in all the East was desperately threatened. Data were sent out from one end of the state to the other, and in October, at the Conservation Forum held in Albany by the Adirondack Mountain Club, more than forty important organizations went on record against the proposal. The forum urged that an emergency committee be formed, and this resulted in the Adirondack Moose River Committee, which now represents nearly a thousand active outdoor and civic groups. Legal counsel has been retained, moving pictures of the region have been duplicated, a speaker's panel has been organized, and an aggressive campaign initiated to attempt, even at a late hour, to retrieve the desperate situation.

Such a flood of protests was sent to the conservation commissioner that he publicly acknowledged his inability to answer letters individually. Sometime later the Black River Regulating District Board, which planned and intends to build the reservoirs, also started sending out mimeographed replies, indicating tremendous pressure. Hundreds of scientists and naturalists, scores of clubs, and thousands of individuals have protested the proposed destruction. Boards of supervisors, fire departments, and chambers of commerce are included in the list of those opposed, as well as such national groups as the Wilderness Society and the National Parks Association.

The issue is reaching a head now, with a bill approved by the Adirondack Moose River Committee and sponsored by the chairman of the conservation committee of the state assembly now before the legislature. This bill would ban all future reservoirs for power purposes in the Adirondacks, except as may in the future be approved by the legislature, with the provisions of the constitutional restriction. At a public hearing in the state capitol on February 27, 1946, more than thirty groups—representing nearly a thousand clubs—appeared in favor of the bill, while but two public agencies and one sportsmen's club opposed it. Conservationists are not yet hopeful of complete success, but they are leaving no stone unturned to save this region.

Of course we shall have to battle for the solitude of the forests which clothe our peaks, for the purity of our rivers born among the crags and sweeping majestically down through peaceful valleys, and for the peace and tranquillity of the beautiful glacial lakes which lie tucked amid these ancient hills.

It will be a constant, ceaseless battle, requiring courage and vigilance down through the years. Once again we should be alarmed lest the things we treasure so greatly be lost in the thoughtless, heedless rush of modern mechanized civilization. If we are tempted to be discouraged at the prospect, we should recall the odds faced by the twenty-five-year-old Verplanck Colvin in 1872. Then millions of acres of state land had been sold for a few cents an acre, or stolen from it, until only thirty-eight thousand acres out of more than five million remained in state ownership. The whole mountain system was in the hands of the despoiler and was being pillaged and burned. There were no forest protective laws, no park administration, no fish and game laws. The lands were largely uncharted and, generally speaking, unknown to the people of the state. Verplanck Colvin was savagely attacked by political interests in behalf of the commercial barons who decried public knowledge of the lands before full exploitation of them could be made. His pay as chief of the Adirondack Survey was withheld from him for long periods of time during which he had to draw on his own resources to pay bills incurred as a state official. But Colvin had the vision and faith that the land could yet be saved. And much of it was.

Now we have mountain clubs and conservation associations, sportsmen and the general public supporting our position. Now we have with us men with vision, and we have the youth of New York State willing to fight for the land they love so well! It is undoubtedly true that we are faced with more critical problems than at any similar period in the last half century, yet we now know that if the issues at stake can be made clear to our people there will be no question of our ultimate success.

Bob Marshall, Mount Marcy, and the Wilderness

Mount Marcy is located in the midst of a jumble of high peaks in the northeastern Adirondack Mountains of New York State. More than a mile high, its upper slopes well above timberline, it is located seven miles from the nearest point of access and is wild and rugged. The trails to it thread through heavy coniferous and mixed hardwood forests and are steep and spectacular. A favorite trail goes through the precipitous Avalanche Pass, skirts Avalanche Lake and goes under huge blocks of rock broken off the towering cliffs above. The region abounds in streams and waterfalls.

Marcy is composed of rocks about as ancient as any on earth, and its storm-swept summit is scarred by glaciers of the ice age. This mountain provides magnificent views of hundreds of square miles of wild-forest land, including most of the forty-six peaks exceeding four thousand feet in height and more than two thousand lesser mountains, which roll off to the horizon in all directions. Scores of glacial lakes fill the hollows of mountains and valleys which surround Marcy. Just below the summit, on its western shoulder, nestles tiny Lake Tear-of-the-Clouds, ultimate source of the Hudson River. Panther Gorge, with its almost sunless rain forest, drops sharply nearly two thousand feet below its eastern shoulder. This is the land of the white-tail deer, the black bear, the beaver, the fisher, the otter, and the lynx. Here also are the pileated woodpecker, the grouse, the owls, the hermit thrush, and speckled trout. Ferns, mosses, and a rich variety of wilderness flowers grow in profusion.

Into this wild setting one summer day in 1932 strode Bob Mar-

Reprinted, with changes, from the *Living Wilderness*, Summer 1966, by permission of The Wilderness Society.

Mount Marcy and Lake Tear-of-the-Clouds. On this mountain, on July 15, 1932, two wilderness trails converged—one from the Arctic and one from the forest fire at Tahawus. Photograph courtesy of NYS Department of Environmental Conservation.

shall, fresh from several years in the Arctic. The Adirondacks were Bob's first love. He and his brother George and his guide Herb Clark first climbed all the forty-six High Peaks, including many trailless ones, before scarcely anyone else had even thought of it. His father was Louis Marshall, renowned constitutional lawyer noted for his pioneering defense of the Adirondack wilderness. The archives of the Association for the Protection of the Adirondacks, organized in 1901, are filled with letters and accounts of Louis Marshall's work with governors, legislators, and members of constitutional conventions to which he was a delegate, who sought his counsel. He was a prime mover in the defense of New York's constitutional guarantee of its forest preserve.

Before returning from the Arctic, Bob had decided to renew his acquaintance with the Adirondacks at his first opportunity. So, with the gusto that only he could muster, he decided to see how many High Peaks he could climb in a single day and how many vertical feet he could achieve in the process. Beginning at 3:30 A.M. on July 15, 1932, he climbed fourteen peaks totaling 13,600 feet by 10:00 P.M. It was on that day, and under these unique circumstances, that I met Bob Marshall. It was a meeting measured in minutes, yet of immeasurable significance to my life.

Robert Cromie and I had come to the summit of Mount Marcy from North River Mountain where we had photographed the devastation of a forest fire. The fire, caused by lumbering operations, had destroyed much of the Opalescent River country. Our tripod was set on the highest rock, and we were photographing the High Peaks country with a camera loaned to us by Nobel Prize chemist Dr. Irving Langmuir, a devoted friend of the forest preserve.

To combat a proposed constitutional amendment which would have permitted cabin colonies anywhere on state land, we were making a movie of beauty and devastation in the Adirondack Park. The state legislature had twice passed the "closed cabin" proposal, and it was to come before the people in referendum that November. Our strategy was directed by John S. Apperson, the foremost advocate of that era for the maintenance of the preserve's constitutional protection. The Mohawk Valley Hiking Club, of which we were members, had been leading the crusade for about a year. We had traveled all over the state, distributed countless pamphlets and were preparing for a series of public forums before election day.

When we arrived at the summit we found Herb Clark, an Adirondack guide. He carried a lunch for Marshall who was due momentarily. It was about one o'clock when we looked down the steep, rocky, eastern slope of Marcy and saw a tiny figure emerge from the conifers half a mile below. Bob was moving rapidly, and in a little while he bounded over the last rocks to the summit.

He greeted the guide and came over to us with a wide, welcoming smile. "I'm Bob Marshall," he said, shaking our hands with an iron grip. His eyes reflected a great joy for living, and his face was deeply tanned and ruddy with health. He was dressed in a light, well-worn, plaid shirt, blue denims, and sneakers.

We explained the cabin referendum to him and outlined the problems of public apathy. He grasped the situation at once. Perhaps our appearance underscored our earnestness; we were heavy with beard, unkempt, and blackened with the char of the forest fire.

Munching his lunch, he seated himself on the rock summit. As we spoke he seemed to be chafing at the bit. A strong, cool wind whipped his hair. He exuded a restless, dynamic strength of purpose—a strength that had been nurtured in the remote Arctic wilderness.

"But this is only part of the Adirondack problems," I told him. Getting up, we walked to the western side of the peak where we could look down on Mount Adams, about six miles away. "They're stripping Adams of its virgin spruce, clear to the top. Three hundred lumberjacks," I informed him. "And over there—see the burned lands of the Opalescent? It was a crown fire. It leapt Sanford Lake and the river and burned deep, clear to the summit of North River Mountain."

Bob was shocked. "Before I left for the Arctic," he said, "they promised us there would be no more cutting above twenty-five-hundred-feet elevation. Those are the most critical watershed forests in the Adirondacks. The Opalescent River valley was one of the loveliest we had and abundant with wildlife." He was plainly upset. He walked back and forth across the summit and circled it several times, in deep contemplation.

"We simply must band together—all of us who love the wilderness. We must fight together—wherever and whenever wilderness is attacked. We must mobilize all of our resources, all of our energies, all of our devotion to the wilderness. To fail to do this is to permit the American wilderness to be destroyed. That must not happen!"

"Good luck," he said. "I'll do all I can as soon as I get back to Washington. We must keep in contact." He shook hands again and turned toward the valley. "Come on, Herb," he said to the guide.

With that he was off, loping swiftly and easily down the steep mountainside. We watched them. The guide picked his way carefully among the rocks and pockets of above-timberline flowers, scattered like a patchwork quilt on the open slopes. Bob quickly reached timberline. Just before he entered the forest he turned toward us and waved his hand sharply. Then he was gone.

Bob Cromie and I distinctly remember that moment. We were acutely conscious of having met a dynamic personality. He seemed to personify all that we saw before us: the limitless sweep of mountains rolling on and on to far horizons, the ancient rocks, the deep gorges, the unbroken forests, the scores of glacial lakes sparkling in the sunlight, and the rivers threading their way down through lovely valleys. There was about him the essence of a wild freedom and an utter determination to preserve wilderness for generations yet to come. Years later, he expressed in finest prose the sentiments he spoke to us that day:

> The universe of the wilderness, all over the United States, is vanishing with appalling rapidity. It is melting away like the last snowbank on some south-facing mountainside during a hot afternoon in June. It is disappearing while most of those who care more for it than anything else in this world are trying desperately to rally and save it.

We gathered our equipment together and headed down the mountain. We camped that night near Bushnell Falls, and around our open campfire we discussed our experiences of the day. We sensed at the time that this casual meeting foreshadowed more important events. Were we to be part of the "mobilization of all who love the wilderness"? Had we anticipated such mobilization?

Next morning we stopped at Johns Brook Lodge in the valley. Bob Marshall was there. We sat in the warm sun and reminisced. He told us about the Arctic for which he already had a certain nostalgia. We discussed problems of the wilderness. I seem to recall his viewpoints clearly:

> Wilderness and roads are incompatible. The encroachment of roads into wilderness areas often goes by unnoticed until suddenly we find a mechanized vehicle already at a hitherto quiet and lovely wilderness lake. The gradual improvement of footpaths into wider trails invites mechanized use if there is no one on hand at the time to object. Hundreds of miles of improved trails of this kind penetrate into the very heart of many of our most remote regions. As I see it, control of the use of these trails is the heart of the wilderness problem in the Adirondacks.

Coming back to the immediate issue before us, we discussed it at length. He agreed to implement numerous phases of our work, and we left with mutual pledges of assistance.

That same day, probably at the lodge, he wrote a vivid account of his high peak adventure of the previous day. It was published in the October 1932 issue of *High Spots,* official magazine of The Adirondack Mountain Club. It included the following statement: "I had wondered whether, after three summers and a winter of exploration in Arctic Alaska, I could still recapture any of the sense of wilderness I had always gotten from Mount Haystack. Gloriously enough, I did. It was still possible to forget the automobiles and machinery of the present in the vista from this rocky summit from which only in the extreme distance could any signs of man's meddlesome ways be observed."

He followed that with an excellent article entitled "The Perilous Plight in the Adirondack Wilderness." This was published in *High Spots* just before the referendum came to a vote.

A few weeks later the people of New York State sustained our position by a vote of 1,326,000 to 690,000. On January 17, 1933, I received a letter from Bob in which he expressed gratification at the results of the referendum and concluded by saying: "I hope we may meet again some day soon—perhaps on the top of Santanoni Mountain next time."

Four years later, on January 17, 1937, Bob called a meeting of New York members of The Wilderness Society, which had formally come into being in 1935. Among those present were Bob, George Marshall, James Marshall, Raymond Torrey, Arnold Knauth, John S. Apperson, Robert Sterling Yard, and myself. Bob appointed several of us to a "Truck Trail Committee."

As the years passed, the threat of mechanized invasion of the forest preserve became more menacing. Gradually many of the most remote regions were being penetrated by jeeps and other forms of mechanized travel. After the war years, this was accelerated.

Those of us who saw what was happening were not idle; but, for years, it looked as though we were waging a losing battle despite what seemed to be a clear mandate in the constitution to preserve the wilderness character of the region. Finally we made an all-out presentation to the Joint Legislative Committee on Natural Resources for New York State, of which I was an advisory member.

Action began on a small scale when Conservation Commissioner Sharon J. Mauhs closed the Siamese Ponds trail to motorized vehicles. Gradually the tempo was built up. The Association for the Protection of the Adirondacks led the supporting action on this issue. The Adirondack Mountain Club and The Izaak Walton League joined forces. Finally the New York State Conservation Council threw its power behind the effort. Senator Robert Watson Pomeroy, Chairman of the Natural Resources Committee, was of inestimable help.

On December 1, 1965, the conservation commissioner issued regulations protecting nearly one million acres of the forest preserve from motor vehicles and aircraft in the larger wilderness regions. Also some five hundred lakes outside these areas were protected from planes and motorboats. The order was a long step in the right direction; it by no means accomplishes the whole job.

Bob Marshall clearly saw the whole picture more than thirty years ago. He had the kind of vision we need today.

The philosophy he advocated is the only one that can permanently preserve the wilderness. It is the mobilization of all of those forces that care for wilderness; it is eternal vigilance and a determination that this is a resource which must be preserved as a heritage for future generations.

I cannot think of a more appropriate way to conclude these memories of Bob Marshall than to recall a few more of his words:

> To countless people the wilderness provides the ultimate delight because it combines the thrills of jeopardy and beauty. It is the last stand for that glorious adventure into the physically unknown that was commonplace in the lives of our ancestors, and has always constituted a major factor in the happiness of many exploratory souls. It is also the perfect esthetic experience because it appeals to all of the senses. . . . It is vast panoramas, full of height and depth and glowing color, on a scale so overwhelming as to wipe out the ordinary meaning of dimensions. It is the song of the hermit thrush at twilight and the lapping of waves on the shoreline and the melody of the wind in the trees. It is the unique odor of balsams and of freshly turned humus and of mist rising from mountain meadows. It is the feel of spruce needles underfoot and sunshine in your face and wind blowing through your hair. It is all of these at the same time, blended into a unity that can only be appreciated with leisure and which is ruined with artificiality.

Howard Zahniser at Hanging Spear Falls. "How absolutely fitting are these place-names . . . Hanging Spear Falls . . . Opalescent River"—Howard Zahniser, 1946. Photograph courtesy of The Wilderness Society.

To Hanging Spear Falls with Zahnie

Hanging Spear Falls and the Opalescent River climax the wildest and most spectacular river source in the Adirondack Mountains. Near the heart of the High Peak wilderness, this crystal clear-stream is a beginning of the majestic Hudson River which rises on Mount Marcy about five miles upstream and two thousand feet higher than the falls.

The Hanging Spear, which is the final drop of a cataract about six hundred feet high, epitomizes the wild character of New York State's 2.6 million-acre forest preserve. Above the cataract is a lovely sheet of water called the Flowed Lands at elevation 2,763 feet above the sea. To understand elevations in the Adirondacks, it is well to keep in mind the fact that Lake Champlain, which borders the park for more than one hundred miles on the east, is but 95 feet above sea level. Mount Marcy, about twenty-five miles away, rises 5,251 feet above this lake.

Close by the Flowed Lands is Livingston Pond, deep and dark, bordered by virgin cedars. A short distance easterly is Lake Colden and another half mile away is Avalanche Lake. These three mountain lakes, totaling over two miles in length, are hemmed in by precipitous four-to five-thousand-foot peaks. Virgin spruce and other evergreens heavily clothe the lower slopes, gradually diminishing in size, until on the higher elevations they run into alpine conditions above timberline.

On August 8, 1946, Howard Zahniser, Edmund Richard, and I shouldered our packs at Heart Lake, which is in the valley not too far from Lake Placid, and headed up the steep trail to Avalanche Pass on the way to our destination—the Hanging Spear. Zahniser, or Zahnie as he was often called, was then Executive Secretary of the Wilderness So-

Reprinted, with changes, from the *Living Wilderness*, Winter 1970–71, by permission of The Wilderness Society.

ciety and Editor of its publication, the *Living Wilderness*. We had met for the first time several months earlier at a national wildlife conference in New York City, where I had presented a pictorial program designed to help save the Moose River from destruction by Higley Mountain and Panther Mountain dams. The lights had scarcely been turned on after the presentation when Howard introduced himself. He indicated a strong desire to see the Adirondacks, and then and there we had made plans for such a trip. And this was it.

As we eased our packs onto great blocks of stone which cluttered the pass at Avalanche Lake, it was an hour later and we were a thousand feet higher. Cliffs of great mountains rise sharply from this narrow cleft and the clarity of echoes here was almost startling.

The trail is very rough in this area: it goes under, over, and around the huge chunks of cliffs broken from above. At this point Ed, who is an Adirondack guide, successfully complained of lightfootedness and convinced us both to let him tote an unequal load. "I've just got to get in shape for carrying deer this fall," he said. And like most guides (despite a background of college and successful business), he spat tobacco to emphasize his point.

It was a fine experience for me to be walking down spruce and balsam trails with men like Zahnie and Ed. The falls were really not more of an objective than every foot we were traversing. For this was the Adirondack Forest Preserve, one of the most spectacular parts of it. This particular section contains about 250,000 acres of the preserve, including dozens of peaks exceeding four thousand feet, many lakes, and the sources of numerous rivers. Here are a few excerpts from Zahnie's diary written on that day:

> Paul, I, and Ed (in our hiking order) started off on one of the best trips I have ever had, in spite of the fact that I had more trouble than ever. . . . The sciatic nerve in my left hip and leg was excruciating at times. We hiked about eight miles up a fine trail, leading first toward the summit of Mt. Marcy, then along Marcy Brook past Avalanche Pass which is in between stupendous cliffs. Looking across it, we saw the mass of stone of Mt. Colden at this point, with its famous Trap Dike, and on one far end of it saw the debris of the great slide that gives the lake its name. We continued past Lake Colden: the sun reflected in our eyes throwing the MacIntyre Range across the lake from us in a beautiful light. We crossed the Opalescent River [Feldspar Brook] at the end of Lake Colden and followed a trail along the northwest border of the Flowed Lands

and then a little way up Calamity Brook to a lean-to where we made camp and had dinner. While Paul and Ed were trying out the fishing, I set up my tripod and took some pictures. The roll must have been short, for in winding it I ran out of cartridge. After a dinner of pork chops, apple sauce, hard-boiled egg, toast, coffee, and lots of grapefruit juice, we moved our camp over to another lean-to—Flowed Lands lean-to. It is a wonderfully, beautifully situated camp at the water's edge, twenty feet or so above the water, looking out through the trunks of spruce, canoe birch, silver birch and across the tips of small spruce, balsam fir, and mountain ash to MacIntyre Range on the left distance and Colden across from it in the right distance and Avalanche Pass in the center distance. I took the film out of the camera in my sleeping bag, only to find that the new film did not operate right. More trouble to make the scene seem all the more lovely. . . . We talked in front of our campfire and went to sleep in our bags about 11:00.

Our conversation, from the time we started up the trail until about dark, was almost entirely about wilderness. We discussed the genesis of the Adirondack Park through the efforts of Verplanck Colvin, its development up through the years to the Constitutional Convention of 1894, and the passage of the "forever wild" article.

We discussed the almost constant attacks made upon this article by commercial interests seeking water power, timber, or other resources. All of the major attacks had been repulsed, usually by an overwhelming vote of the people. Zahnie was amazed to learn that for the first thirty-seven years of the constitutional protection, the people of the city of New York almost single-handedly maintained the integrity of the forest preserve. Time after time, upstate New York voted for commercializing the public lands; time after time the plurality of the metropolitan vote overcame and defeated the proposed exploitations. In 1932 the trend of upstate voting changed and since then it has maintained its strong support of the "forever wild" clause.

Zahnie was steeped in the early adventures of Bob and George Marshall and the tradition of wilderness preservation they had brought from New York to Washington. Now he began to realize the depth of their commitment and why they so vigorously championed the wilderness. He had not realized the vastness and the extent of the wild forest country of the Adirondacks; nor had he realized the size of the park, which exceeds in size the state of Massachusetts by two thousand square miles.

I had hardly known Zahnie's predecessor, Robert Sterling Yard, editor of the *Living Wilderness*, and I was, of course, very much interested in the man who was to carry the torch lit by Bob Marshall. I think Ed Richard aptly described our first reaction to Zahnie when, soon after we had started this trip, he remarked to me on the side, "He sure can ask questions!" Zahnie asked good, penetrating questions that got right to the root of the matter and was not satisfied with a half-answer. We both felt that he had a patience built on impatience. "We can save the significant parts of the American Wilderness," he said, "if we don't waste time doing it."

During the day, we had hardly mentioned our main Adirondack battle—the threat that Higley Mountain and/or Panther Mountain dams would destroy the Moose River wilderness. But we got to it that night. Ed and I had initiated the fight about a year and a half earlier, after I had been alerted to the threat by George Marshall in New York City. These reservoirs would penetrate to the heart of an area of nearly one thousand square miles not bisected by road. At that time much of it was private land; today, a great deal more of that country has been acquired by the state. It is a land of forests and lakes, with few high mountains, and has wonderful habitat for wildlife, especially the deer. What we needed now was nationwide support—the kind of support that Bob Marshall had in mind when he helped to found The Wilderness Society.

As a matter of fact, within five miles of our campfire, on Mount Marcy's summit, Bob had voiced words to me in 1932 which became an indelible part of my thinking. And here, under a starlit sky in the very shadow of that mountain, was one, who, like Bob Marshall, was a wilderness preserver in his own right, suggesting national strategy to help us in our efforts to save the Adirondacks.

A whole new battle to preserve the South Branch of the Moose River began that night. No longer would a handful of New Yorkers be pitted alone against the most powerful commercial interests in their state. Now there were also people like Dr. Ira Gabrielson and Carl Gutermuth of the Wildlife Management Institute, Anthony Wayne Smith, then Chief Counsel and Chairman of the Conservation and Development Committee of the CIO (Congress of Industrial Organizations), David Brower, then of the Sierra Club, Devereux Butcher, then of the National Parks Association, and many others who would forcefully join the fray. And they did! All that Zahnie said he would do, he did, and so much more that it can never be equaled!

Today, more than twenty years later, the South Branch of the Moose River still flows unobstructed down through lovely avenues of ancient evergreens; the Indian River still adds its tribute to the Moose through banks of fern by its still waters; the deer still have their winter-yarding grounds on the fabled Moose River Plains, where all was to have been transformed into cemeteries of stumps and dreary mud flats!

About 10:30 we stopped talking about wilderness and just soaked it in. Shadows from our blazing campfire flickered and danced on the trees around us; occasionally an owl hooted off in the woods, and a warm breeze from the south brought us the sound of the falls of the Hanging Spear. We reminisced about other such campfires and made plans for more like this. The full richness of Zahnie's personality came into our lives there: the smile that began in his eyes, the faith in his and our cause, his family happiness, and his almost limitless reservoir of friends concerned with our American heritage—we now became a part of all this. The day had been long and rewarding, the morrow would soon be here . . .

We were awake at dawn and from our sleeping bags we watched the sun fire the fifty-one hundred foot-high Algonquin Peak and gradually light the evergreens downward to the lake. It was to be another perfect day, when the momentous things of life were again to be the joy of good friends on the trail, the music of water lapping a wild shoreline, the chatter of a red squirrel, and stillness accentuated by the occasional song of a thrush or veery, or the shrill cry of a hawk wheeling high in the sky above us.

After breakfast we went down the trail in back of camp toward Hanging Spear Falls. This is extremely wild and dramatic country. Parallel to the rapids and white waters above the final and highest falls, the trail pitches steeply down through spruces and balsams. A sharp bend in the trail revealed a ledge from which a fine view of the falls could be seen from well above it. We made our way down to its base and the great pool there. Zahnie enjoyed the wild splendor of the scene—the solitude, the remoteness, the roar of water, the jumble of cliffs clothed with ferns and mosses and with evergreens clinging to narrow ledges and crannies in rocks. And in the center of this dark gorge were the sun-drenched falls, sparkling with crystal-clear water fed by our most elevated mountain lakes and springs. "How absolutely fitting are these place names," he remarked, "the Hanging Spear, on the Opalescent River."

We tarried at length there, luxuriating in the warm sunshine, feeling the texture of these most ancient rocks, and enjoying the lush ferns and mosses and occasional flowers. We spoke very little there, and when it was time to leave, we did so most reluctantly.

Back at the lean-to, we enjoyed our final meal. Then Zahnie went down to the water's edge and sat in the sun with his feet in the water. After a while, I joined him. "I've been trying to make a comparison of this view to some other one I know," he said, "but there's nothing else I've ever seen quite like it. It has the same kind of perfection I sensed when looking at the Grand Tetons." And then, getting up, he looked once again up the valley toward Avalanche Pass. "So this was Bob Marshall's country," he remarked. "No wonder he loved it so!"

We packed and started our five-mile hike down Calamity Brook toward the Tahawus Club, a small cluster of darkly stained summer homes tucked about a dozen miles up in the woods at the end of the road, occupied by descendants of the early explorers. We passed Calamity Pond, where one of these men accidentally shot himself nearly a century before. Several hours later we reached the Henderson River and Ed's car, driven by Mrs. Zahniser, who had agreed to meet us at the end of our fifteen-mile hike, at a spot which was more than sixty miles by road from our starting place.

Happily for us, he fell in love with the country and soon had a cabin situated on an east-facing mountain slope close to the Siamese Ponds wilderness. Located at the end of the road, overlooking Crane Mountain and the east central Adirondacks, it was a haven for him and his family which he came to as frequently as possible, to rest from exhausting forays in Washington. Here he could dream a little and plan new strategies for the protection of wilderness. He could also take a trail from his backdoor and immediately be in a block of state forest preserve comprising more than a hundred thousand acres, replete with splendid forests, fifty lakes, innumerable streams, and waterfalls, and all that goes to make up land protected from the commercial incursions of man.

I was privileged to have many hours with him here and in the nearby wilderness. We climbed numerous mountains from which we could see thousands of square miles of the Adirondacks as well as the Green Mountains beyond Lake Champlain, the High Peaks about forty miles north, and, on very clear days, Canada beyond the Saint Lawrence River to the north, and the Catskill Mountains a hundred miles to the south.

One of his conversations with Ed and me on the trip was most significant in light of future events. He said, "In addition to such protection as national parks and monuments are now given, we need some strong legislation which will be similar in effect on a national scale to what Article XIV, Section 1, is to the New York State Forest Preserve.

Alice and Howard Zahniser at their Adirondack cabin. There at the end of the trail, where the wilderness begins, the National Wilderness Preservation Act crystallized. Photograph reprinted by permission of Alice B. Zahniser.

We need to reclaim for the people, perhaps through their representatives in the Congress, control over the wilderness regions of America."

Twenty years later, thanks largely to his dedication and indefatigable spirit, this dream became a reality. On September 3, 1964, four months after Zahnie's death, Lyndon Johnson, president of the United States, affixed his signature to the National Wilderness Preservation Act, which automatically protected a little more than nine million acres of our nation's most cherished lands.

Wilderness Preservation System Hearing

MRS. PFOST: Our next witness will be Mr. Paul Schaefer, director of the New York State Conservation Council. He is representing the Association for the Protection of the Adirondacks and the Friends of the Forest Preserve.

For the benefit of committee members, we are going out of order momentarily to turn to him, because he has a plane reservation, and he must leave the committee room in a few minutes. We will hear him so he can keep his appointment in New York.

STATEMENT OF PAUL SCHAEFER, DIRECTOR
NEW YORK STATE CONSERVATION COUNCIL
TROY, N.Y.

MR. SCHAEFER: Madam Chairman, members of the committee, thank you very much for your consideration.

I have the honor to represent Robert Watson Pomeroy, chairman of the Joint Legislative Committee on Natural Resources for New York State. He has asked me, and he has also asked Congressman Wharton, to put these remarks in the record today. Mr. Pomeroy would be here himself except for reorganization of the New York State Legislature today.

As chairman of the committee, he says this:

> In my capacity as chairman of the Joint Legislative Committee on Natural Resources of the State of New York, and on behalf

U.S. House Committee on Interior and Insular Affairs, *Wilderness Preservation System Hearing,* May 7–11, 1962 [Ser. no. 12 pt. 4, pp. 1308–12]. Washington: Government Printing Office, 1962.

of such committee, I strongly urge favorable action by your sub-committee on the wilderness bill, S.174, now before it for consideration.

New York was a pioneer in the preservation of wilderness in the East. In 1885 the legislature established our forest preserve and gave it statutory protection by the provision that: "The lands (of the state) now or hereafter constituting the forest preserve shall be forever kept as wild forest lands. They shall not be sold nor shall they be leased or taken by any corporation, public or private."

By now the preserve has grown to two and one-half million acres. While it consists of many separate blocks of land lying in both the Adirondack and Catskill mountain regions, it nevertheless includes some which are both large and remote, containing no roads or permanent buildings. Sixteen of such areas range in size from over 14,000 to over 180,000 acres. Areas in the New York State Forest Preserve are, with very few exceptions, the only public lands in the United States east of the Mississippi River which, in size and remoteness, can qualify as wilderness.

The physical, sociological, and political aspects of the forest preserve in the Adirondacks and Catskills have been the subject of extensive study by the Joint Legislative Committee on Natural Resources for eleven years. During the past three years, in which I have had the honor to serve as its chairman, the committee has given particular attention to the preservation of its unique wilderness character.

A review of the history of the preserve, and the study of its present-day public use and management problems, reveal many similarities between the experiences of New York State and those of the Congress of the United States in their respective efforts to preserve our heritage of wilderness. I list herewith some of the lessons learned in New York for your consideration in determining proper action on S.174:

1. The forest preserve has become a great economic asset to the state. It brings thousands of new campers, hikers, hunters, and fishermen to the Adirondacks and Catskills each year. What attracts them? The natural splendor of the scenery all around them —the opportunity to find peace and quiet away from the hubbub of the world and to be in touch with the timeless wonders of nature.

It is not necessary to climb a mountain to be thrilled by its scenic beauty or to feel the awe it inspires. But a mountain that thousands can "climb" in the comfort and ease of a motor vehicle no longer commands the same reverence; no longer inspires the same awe.

2. The strongest statutory protection is imperative if wilderness areas are to be successfully protected from commercial exploitation.

In New York State, the mere passage of laws by the legislature in 1885 were not enough. By 1894, one-eighth of the forest preserve land had been lost to the state and an enormous amount of standing timber had been sold, even against the judgment of the state engineer and surveyor.

The people of New York, in their disgust, then took the matter into their own hands and placed the preserve under the protection of the state constitution, which, as you know, reads as follows: "The lands of the state now owned or hereafter acquired constituting the forest preserve as now fixed by law shall be forever kept as wild forest lands. They shall not be leased, sold, or exchanged, or be taken by any corporation, public nor private, nor shall the timber thereon be sold, removed, or destroyed." Since the constitution was enacted in 1895, many attempts have been made to break through this constitutional protection. Never, however, have the people allowed it. Though certain specific exceptions in the use of the preserve have been permitted, every attack on the basic principles of protection has been aggressively fought and rejected. The people realize that the great economic and human values of the preserve can survive only if the strongest possible protection is maintained around it.

3. Just as present-day life brings greater need for wilderness, so do modern travel facilities, and longer vacation periods bring ever increasing use of it, wherever it exists. The New York State Conservation Department has estimated that three million man-days use was made of the foot trails and lean-tos leading into the forest preserve and its remote areas last year. This figure belies the contention, for our state, at least, that the creation and preservation of wilderness means the setting aside of great, extensive areas of land for only a small minority. Nor was the use of these trails confined to those in the prime of their vigor. Many of the old and very young have also been found among those who hike through the mountains and climb the trails on them.

4. Motorized transportation is incompatible with wilderness. Easy means of access reduces or obliterates the awe and reverence for wilderness. Jeeps and other motorized ground vehicles churn footpaths into quagmires, motorboats spoil canoeing, and the landing of airplanes and helicopters on a wilderness pond can ruin the solitude and beauty of a fisherman's paradise. And all such motorized transportation means more unsightly litter and greater fire hazard.

The wilderness bill, S.174, now before your honorable sub-committee, contains adequate insurance that no mineral or forest resource will be irretrievably lost or kept from use or development if the actual need should arise. It will also serve to guard the irreplaceable wilderness resource of our nation against needless commercial exploitation. Thus it will help to preserve for future generations a great heritage and tradition of our country.

I strongly urge your favorable action on this bill.

Madam Chairman, I have the privilege of representing the New York State Conservation Council and the Association for the Protection of the Adirondacks. I would briefly sum up our position as this:

The people of New York State understand the value of wilderness and have proved this by the fact that they possess 2.5 million acres of wild-forest land in the Adirondack and Catskill mountains. Further, since 1895, they have given their public domain extraordinary protection by the constitutional provision requiring that the land be kept as forest land.

Efforts to modify this have been signally unsuccessful during the past sixty-seven years. Time after time, such efforts have been defeated by the people in referendum, and they have, in sharp contrast, backed all moves to enlarge and enhance their forest preserve.

Presently they are spending $7.5 million for the forest preserve, and the 1962 legislature has just approved an important additional bond issue for this purpose.

This is so because there is a growing awareness of the need in New York and elsewhere for extensive regions where natural conditions will always remain unmodified by man; where one can find peace and tranquillity, and free oneself occasionally from the turmoils and artificialities of our complex civilization. Wilderness is not a luxury; it is a dire necessity in this age and will become ever more precious as the years go on.

It should be no surprise, therefore, to find virtually all conservation and sportsmen's organizations in New York State solidly in back of this legislation.

The New York State Conservation Council with its twelve hundred clubs and 300,000 members, the Association for the Protection of the Adirondacks, the Izaak Walton League, the Adirondack Mountain Club, and innumerable others all join in support of the Wilderness Act, S.174.

I am sure that I speak for hundreds of New York organizations and hundreds of thousands of individuals when I say we expect this 87th Congress to enact this legislation without delay or weakening amendments.

The journey to this public hearing has been, for those genuinely concerned with the preservation of the American wilderness, long and arduous. May we, therefore, with every consideration for the problems you must face, express our sincere hope that your honorable body will report favorably on S.174.

I am confident that such a decision will be hailed by the American people and will represent one of the most significant and valuable achievements by the United State Congress in the history of our nation.

Thank you very much.

I want to end by saying, Mrs. Pfost, that I am sure that the eyes of the nation are on your committee, and we are looking forward with great confidence to the favorable action by your group to preserve this magnificent country for all generations. Thank you very much.

MRS. PFOST: Thank you, Mr. Schaefer.

6

The Forest Preserve

THE PEOPLE'S LAND

Cataract on Eleventh Mountain. A high mountain ledge, the music of falling water, a rainbow in the mist . . . is this site not an ultimate of creation?

Success on many issues related to the Adirondacks and Catskills enabled many of us to speak with some authority when we presented viewpoints to a constitutional convention, to state agencies, congress, or to state and national organizations.

During the more than half a century of activities, scores of diverse issues surfaced threatening the integrity of the New York State Forest Preserve. Often the proposals were backed by entrenched commercial interests with almost unlimited financial resources. Twice our adversaries were the associated industries of the state, the New York State Conference of Mayors, and the United States Army Corps of Engineers. We lost numerous skirmishes but never a war. In the process, we had known the depths of despair and then the exhilaration of victory. In the end, on issue after issue, our patience and persistence won over the hearts of the people, and with that, the legislature and the various media.

The successes we knew came about only by the cooperation of hundreds of organizations and thousands of individuals who poured their time and often their money into supporting our ideals. Such successes could not have come about if there did not exist that ideal—the "forever wild" covenant in the New York State Constitution.

East Branch of the Sacandaga River. Here is a universe older than history, where nature has full reign.

The Ad-i-ron-dac

It would take more than the genius of a poet to adequately describe the full meaning of the word "Adirondack" to those of us who have answered the irresistible call of these mountains. The spell of the land comes quickly over one as one walks down the fragrant forest trail to the tiny lake tucked away in the peaceful hills, or as he climbs up the last precipitous rock to the wild windswept peak and stands breathless at the infinite sea of mountains that roll away to far horizons.

It is all too true that parts of the Adirondacks have been pillaged and burned and plundered, and that problems are continually arising which defy patience and demand the most exacting and tireless activity by those who would preserve a vestige of the former glory of this land. But it is also true that as a result of the combined efforts of the many who have lifted up their voices in behalf of the mountains we still have much to enjoy and much to appreciate.

More than eighty years ago, John Burroughs described his reactions to a trip in the Boreas River country:

> The woods were Nature's own. It was a luxury to ramble through them, rank and shaggy and venerable, but with an aspect similarly ripe and mellow. No fire had consumed, no lumberman plundered. Every trunk and limb and leaf lay where it had fallen. At every step, the foot sank into the moss, which like a soft green snow, covered everything, making every stone a cushion and every rock a bed—a grand old Norse parlor; adorned beyond art and upholstered beyond skill.

Reprinted from the *Cloudsplitter*, 1944, by permission of The Cloudsplitter, Albany Chapter, ADK.

We still have scenes in the Adirondacks like Burroughs described. We still can obtain, if we will, the priceless elements of untamed nature—the infinite distances, the stupendous cliffs, the emerald lakes, the solitude of the deep forest. The grandeur of Indian Pass may be enjoyed even as it was in 1868 by Alfred Street, the wild beauty of the Kunjamuk we may still see as did Charles Fenno Hoffman in 1839. And each of us can be a Verplanck Colvin, restlessly exploring the high peaks and the dense swamps, the gorge and the cataract, thrilled beyond expression at the gleam of a crystal in the pool at which he stopped to drink, or awed at the fury of the storms, which broke so suddenly over the mountains.

It is unfortunate that so many people are blind to the forces that leave havoc and destruction of natural beauty and resources in their wake, breaking for all time the priceless element of continuity in the work of nature. The burned and ravaged mountains stand in mute but eloquent testimony to man's inhumanity to man—the carelessness of one generation destroying the rightful heritage of a hundred generations. But it is also unfortunate to be blind to the sublime beauty and grandeur that exists so extensively throughout the seven thousand square miles of these mountains.

Like "Adirondack Harry" Radford, whose mother without success took him to the most renowned places of history and art in Europe in the hope of diverting his mind from his beloved mountains, we will always maintain with constancy our personal belief in the unrivaled glory of Lake George, or the wild majesty of Mount Marcy, or the mystical beauty of Miami Swamp, or the exquisite loveliness of the upper Oswegatchie country.

Preservation of the woods and waters is a most natural reaction to enjoyment of them. If the Hudson River runs black, or the forests are threatened or the roads would penetrate, then we must act. For the youth of tomorrow, even as we, will hunger for the simple joys of the forest trail and will need the peace and tranquillity of mind so quickly obtained by mingling with the timeless elements of an abundant nature.

We should count it a privilege to aid in securing this Adirondack heritage!

Forever Wild

When P. W. Fosburgh was the editor of the *New York State Conservationist*, he raised the question as to whether or not the forest preserve in the Adirondacks should be opened to lumbering, it is doubtful if he realized the extent of the reaction against such a proposal as has occurred. His questions were simple and to the point. They were:

1. If our objective is the preservation of our forests, are forests best preserved by prohibiting cutting?

2. What is meant by "forever wild"? Does it suggest an abundance of birds and animals, and if so, does our present management policy promote this objective?

3. How does the present management policy, as prescribed by our constitution, contribute to the economic needs of state and nation?

4. Under this policy, are we making the most of the potential recreational values of the forest preserve?

At least one major thing that perhaps the editor of the conservation department's publication overlooked is that members of the Joint Legislative Committee on River Regulation for New York State have just spent almost three years of mind-searching on these very questions.

Admittedly such a committee, headed by the honorable John L. Ostrander, which was primarily charged with finding the answers to the explosive Adirondack reservoir problems, might, on the face of things, have little to do with forestry. And yet the committee was but a few months old when Assemblyman Ostrander made the following state-

Reprinted from the *Forest Preserve*, January 1952.

ment: "We now recognize that river regulation begins not in the river and lake valleys but on the uppermost reaches of our mountain peaks."

In the process of getting information to present to the Joint Legislative Committee on River Regulation, we have waded Adirondack rivers and climbed fire-ravaged rocky slopes, and have stood on windswept pinnacles looking down upon tens of thousands of acres of barren, destroyed land. We have also checked the extremely thin soil conditions on numerous mountains and have stood beneath groves of virgin spruces on critical mountain slopes where less than eight inches of soil is all that gives life to these forest giants. We have watched the beginning of the rivers high on the forested peaks where the steady drip of water absorbed from the clouds forms the first crystal spring. And we have felt the matted forest floor, intertwined with millions of roots, move when the storms hit the crowns of the trees guarding the mountain slopes, and realized how dependent each tree with its living roots is upon the other for support.

Then, as these truths became evident to us, the facts were laid before the committee in public meetings in Schenectady, Albany, New York City, Buffalo, Syracuse, Watertown, Cranberry Lake, and other places. A cross section of our best thinkers on the national, as well as the state level, gave testimony and answered questions at these hearings.

Is it any wonder that conservationists should be perhaps a little impatient with the *New York State Conservationist* for raising these questions at a time when the records have been so carefully stated? Of course had a member of the conservation department attended even one of the many public hearings of the legislative committee, he might have sensed the feeling of the people with respect to their forest preserve. He would have heard the plain answer to question No. 2 that asked what is meant by "forever wild," an answer the New York State Court of Appeals ruled on more than twenty years ago and which stipulates that meaning as follows:

> Giving to the phrase "forever kept as wild forest lands" the significance which the term "wild forest" bears, we must conclude that the idea intended was a health resort and playground with the attributes of a wild forest park as distinguished from other parks so common to our civilization. We must preserve it in its wild state, its trees, its rocks, its streams. It was to be a great resort for the free use of the people in which nature is given free rein. Its uses for health and pleasure must not be inconsistent with its preservation as forest lands in a wild state. It must always retain the character of

a wilderness. It is essentially a quiet and healthful retreat from the turmoils and artificialities of a busy urban life.

We would be remiss if we did not indicate the gratitude of hundreds of thousands of the people of New York State in their knowledge that from the concrete canyons of New York City, a clear evaluation of the problem was made via the *New York Times* (November 23, 1951):

> The Adirondack Forest Preserve is not intended to be an area for commercial exploitation, nor is it intended to be a highly developed playground or a manicured park. If the rigid restrictions of the New York State Constitution are ever lifted we may expect within a very few years to see this priceless land of unspoiled natural beauty turned into a "recreational area" with an entirely different set of standards and an entirely different purpose from that which it now fulfills. Despite propaganda to the contrary, the forest preserve is freely open to hikers and campers and those who seek something of the dwindling wildness of our country. It is not a place for concrete bathing pools, luxurious hotels, or superhighways.

We sincerely hope that because of the reactions which are so evident in all parts of the state, the *New York State Conservationist* will from here on take the position editorially that "the lands of the state . . . constituting the forest preserve . . . shall be forever kept as wild forest lands."

High Peaks.

Wild Forest Land

From the summit of Giant Mountain east of Keene Valley to Dry Timber Lake west of the Oswegatchie headwaters is a distance of eighty miles. Nearly one hundred miles lie between the North Branch of the Grass River and Trout Lake in the southern Adirondacks. Incredible though It seems, it was actually possible a scant half century ago to traverse the magnificent mountain and lake country intervening without once having to leave the primeval forest!

Most of the High Peaks region and much of the vast lake country was virtually an unbroken forest in 1895. Most of the easily accessible river and valley lands had been fully exploited by the lumbermen then. The Upper Hudson, the Sacandaga, the Ausable, the Saranac, the Raquette, the Boreas, and the lower Oswegatchie valleys with their matchless forests containing probably the largest and finest trees in eastern America had been cut. Such lakes as Piseco, the Saranacs, Blue Mountain, and Indian had lost their first-growth trees. Others like Long Lake, Big Moose, and Little Tupper still retained much of their original primeval beauty. Here and there a fire had swept over lumbered lands. Sanford Lake, Cheney Pond, Bad Luck Pond, Thirteenth Lake, and similar regions were denuded.

In general the southeastern quarter of the land now within the Adirondack Park, together with several hundred square miles centering around Tupper Lake had been lumbered. The High Peaks region, along with the central and southern interior lands were unspoiled and contained such magnificent trees that even John Burroughs found himself at a loss to portray adequately his emotions as he tramped across the seemingly endless miles of woods. One could walk for days without los-

Friends of the Forest Preserve brochure, September 1953.

205

ing sight of the spires of the ancient forest etched against the sky. The absence of devastation was in particular evidence in the Mount Marcy region.

Verplanck Colvin and his contemporaries were inspired by the existence of these vital headwater forests. They knew that when the lumberman had exploited the forests easily accessible to the rivers which afforded cheap transportation for his logs, he would strip the mountain slopes of their irreplaceable evergreen forests which protected the headwaters of our major rivers and streams. And then he would attack the more remote interior, where hundreds of crystal lakes and ponds still lay in all their primitive glory, undisturbed save by the deer, the bear, or the panther or an occasional hunter lured into these depths by the beauty of this solitude.

In 1891 the area of virgin forest in the Adirondacks was estimated to be 1,932,000 acres. This had dwindled to 1,600,000 acres in 1894 and was being further reduced by about 80,000 acres each year. Such swift destruction of irreplaceable resources was brought out in the New York State Constitutional Convention of 1894, and the need for immediate action to secure watershed protection was made apparent. As a result that unparalleled Article VII, Section 7, was unanimously adopted, declaring that "the lands of the state . . . shall be forever kept as wild forest lands."

In addition to protecting the lands then owned by the state, it was the intention of the authors of this forest-protection legislation to acquire the vital headwater lands before they were lumbered. This objective, unfortunately, was not fully realized, for of the 1.6 million acres of virgin forest then existing, one million acres have since been lumbered. The total virgin forest now existing is estimated to be about 200,000 acres, situated principally in the Raquette Lake region and the Oswegatchie River headwaters. Since both of these areas were in state ownership prior to 1895, it follows that no substantial areas of virgin forest were purchased in the last fifty years, but rather the lands which had been lumbered or burned, or contained forests of little commercial value. The tragedy of this policy is emphasized when such outstanding purchases as the virgin forest in the Moose River valley or the jewel of Paradise Bay on Lake George are seen, and one catches a glimpse of the glory which once covered ten thousand square miles of northern New York.

As was foreseen by Colvin, Edmond C. Martin, Frank S. Gardener, Peter Schofield, and others, the forests not in state ownership melted away with astonishing rapidity. The lumbermen attacked the mountain slopes and peaks with vigor and thereby set the stage for a major Adirondack disaster.

Unusual drought conditions of 1903 brought the archenemy of the woods, forest fire, into front-page prominence. Thousands of fires started all over the Adirondacks. Nearly 500,000 acres burned, including much of the High Peaks region. Again in 1908 similar conditions existed and nearly 400,000 acres burned, In both instances the conflagrations continued until rain or snow put them out, despite the fact that thousands of men used every known method of fire fighting in a futile effort to halt the destruction.

Despite the fact that many of the original objectives of Article VII, Section 7 (changed to Article XIV, Section 1, in 1938), were thwarted, the benefits of this fundamental law have been very great indeed. Today we are reaping the multiple blessings and benefits made possible by the vision of our Adirondack immortals.

A substantial area of Adirondack lands contained a mixed forest of hardwoods, such as beech, birch, and maple, and softwoods such as spruce, pine, hemlock, and balsam. For the most part the lumbermen took only the softwoods, which could be floated down the rivers to the mills. The remaining hardwoods in such mixed forests protected them from fire to a certain extent by shading the forest floor and thereby aiding the slow process of decay of the lumbering debris. After 1895 cutting on state lands automatically stopped. Gradually the softwood stumps rotted away, and a kind of primitive beauty came back to portions of the Adirondacks.

The progressive character of the strict constitutional protection given the forest preserve is brought into sharp relief by the recovery of devastated areas by nature. By simply being left alone, nature has, in from a quarter to a half century, produced from cutover regions, recreational lands unsurpassed in northeastern America. Of course many of the high peaks and scores of lesser ones are irreparably damaged, and centuries must come and go before the forests can come back. But at least the destruction by man has been halted and the processes of nature, including the slow building of soil, have begun.

Not least among the advantages of the existing law is its prohibition of roads on forest preserve lands. To a large extent, the road building since 1895 in the Adirondacks has been confined to existing arteries of traffic, rather than highways that would bisect the remaining wild areas and destroy for all time the wilderness character of portions of the Adirondacks. The unique values of this wilderness character are just being fully realized, as almost all of these wild areas are now included in the forest preserve and as better transportation makes these lands available to more and more of our people.

Increasingly large numbers of people are experiencing for the first time the intangible yet inspiring qualities of wild-forest land. There is every reason to believe that this trend will continue in ever-increasing volume, as thousands each year graduate from the state's public campsites and take their first steps down the winding trails into the interior Adirondacks.

In all the world, what can be of greater moment to the human sensibilities than, after having packed miles along a winding Adirondack trail, to come at last to a ridge from which the crystal waters of a mountain pond can be seen sparkling through the trees?

For here is a universe older than history, over which nature has full reign and man is of little more consequence than the deer, which come to these pure waters from surrounding wooded ridges. For a moment his hand is stayed, as it were, and he neither destroys nor constructs. He has left time behind him, and the mind that conceived death-dealing implements of war, or decided laws to govern his fellows, or fashioned metal or wood for artistic delight comes to a pause in its nerve-wracking journey. For a moment, he becomes as a pebble on the beach and before the exquisite beauties and awesome forces of nature submits himself, to a greater or lesser degree, to these ageless things which link him with the dim and distant past.

All of his senses reawaken. The tramp along the forest trail has prepared him for the leisurely, delightful experience of living simply again. A coordination of inconsequential things gives each moment a strange, new meaning. The bewitching fragrance of the woods, the almost imperceptible wave action on the shore, the distant rumble of a cataract, the glimpse of ancient trees etched against the skyline, the pleasing warmth of the campfire—these things in a land with which man is at peace bring to the mind a tranquillity and a new zest for living.

The unique charm of the Adirondacks as we know them today may be enjoyed only because a half century ago a few men had vision, and the courage and energy to translate such vision into a reality.

This heritage may be retained and increased for the benefit of posterity only if we correctly interpret our responsibility and direct our energies toward the common objective to sustain the immortal declaration that "the lands of the state . . . shall be forever kept as wild forest lands."

The Forest Preserve and
Recreational Needs of the
People of New York State

The New York State Forest Preserve in the Adirondacks and the Catskill Mountains is serving the people of New York State in ways and to a degree that had been scarcely dreamed of a generation ago. During the past several years, such use has accelerated so rapidly that we are finding it difficult to keep up with even the most simple facilities required by the increasing number of citizens who want to make use of the public domain. It is very obvious that a realistic reappraisal of our recreational program must be made and steps taken to realize some of the potentials that exist in these unique mountain regions.

The recreational potential of the forest preserve has hardly been scratched as yet despite all the forward-looking efforts of those administering it and the interests of the public which seeks to use it. Some of the reasons for this fact may be found in the following statements:

1. The land ownership pattern of the forest preserve is very inadequate. Areas with great wilderness value need to be blocked out to make possible good administration by the conservation department. The scattered ownership pattern of the preserve results in constant conflicts of interest and in some cases rules out good public use because of access difficulties. Funds should be made available without further delay for the purchase of key in-holdings when they become available.

Reprinted from a speech delivered to the New York Section of the Society of American Foresters, Albany, New York, April 1965.

Adirondack lean-to. Almost synonymous with the word Adirondack is the picturesque open log lean-to.

2. The ownership by the state of superlative wild-forest lands in the High Peaks and lesser peak regions as well as in the lake country is not sufficiently known by the people of our state. During the eleven years I traveled the length and breadth of the state in our battle against the proposed Higley and Panther Mountain dams in the Moose River country, I found an almost unbelievable lack of knowledge of the forest preserve. For example, the average citizen believes the Adirondack Park may have as many as one hundred lakes. He is amazed when told the number is over two thousand. In like manner, he does not comprehend the fact that the Adirondack Park is larger than any national park in the contiguous states, that it has several thousand mountains, scores of rivers, and almost numberless streams. A program of education as to the vast extent and matchless beauty of this region is, of course, highly desirable.

3. To a degree, the softness of our way of life has in recent years kept the average person close to his automobile.

Recreation, which can not be obtained close to the car, has for a vast majority of people, lost much of its meaning. A good example of this is the fact that only recently have wilderness deer hunting camps been reviving. In one section of the Adirondacks with which I am familiar there were, thirty years ago, deer hunting parties on virtually every wilderness lake in an area of fifty square miles. Ten years ago this had dropped off to a point where virtually none of the lakes were used. The large increase in the number of deer in other parts of the state, plus the fact that they could be obtained along the roads, was responsible for this condition. Now, however, due to the terrific hunting pressure in those areas, wilderness hunting, with its infinitely superior opportunities for well-rounded adventure is coming back, this time to stay.

In contemplating an accelerated program of use of the preserve, it should be kept in mind that under our unique forest-protection instrument, Article XIV, Section 1, of the state constitution, multiple recreational uses are possible under the law. The so-called restrictions have for years been grossly overdrawn. The only way in which the constitution hampers forest recreation is that it keeps commercial ventures out of the public domain. Conversely this policy gives private enterprise great opportunities to establish cabins and other facilities on private lands adjacent to the preserve. Our present forest policy works ideally for the benefit of the woods and automatically creates a quiet, restful atmosphere so essential to our well-being.

Public use of state campsites has increased from 561,888 individuals camping 901,150 days in 1947 to 991,214 individuals camping 1,955,474 days in 1957. Last year more than 90,000 would-be campers were turned away.

These figures are testimony in favor of the New York State Conservation Department's ten-year plan to double the number of campsites in the forest preserve. It is becoming more and more apparent, however, that new campsites, with the heavy concentrations of people, should be constructed along existing paved highways, rather than in semiwild or wilderness regions of the preserve.

There is a growing demand for more informal camping, and it is obvious that semiwild lakes should be reserved to take care of this growing demand.

The forest preserve in the Adirondacks provides the setting for some of the best wilderness hunting in the United States. While the numbers of organized hunting camps are growing, they hardly approach the number of such camps in the early days of the century, if population growth is taken into consideration. There are, of course, more big-game hunters using the region than ever before, but large numbers of them are roadside hunters who seldom penetrate more than a mile or so from the highway.

The best big-game hunting in the Adirondacks, at least from the standpoint of public lands, is in the interior of the larger wilderness tracts.

On this subject, I have had thirty years experience since I began guiding parties of hunters in 1927. While it may be true that elsewhere there are more deer per square mile or places where less effort gets more venison, I am sure that there is no place on earth that affords a more enjoyable or satisfying hunting experience than is obtainable in the forest preserve. Over a period of many years, our parties have averaged about a buck for every two hunters, but we have counted such luck the very least of our hunting success.

What counts is living and hunting in wild, undisturbed-by-man forest land—a land replete with vast distances, quiet forest solitudes, wild rivers, foaming cataracts, and lakes tucked away in forested hills. It is the renewing of our understanding of primitive things, the sharpening of our sensibilities to the loveliness of rocks and sunsets and silence. It is, indeed, experiencing a world we have almost forgotten, a way of life based on personal effort and individual initiative—whether the problem be the penetration of a trackless swamp, the climbing of a wild windswept peak, or merely reflection on our way of life in an environment that invites such penetrating thoughts.

There are vast opportunities for more people to use the forest preserve for wilderness hunting.

In years gone by, the Adirondack and Catskill trout fishing was world-renowned. Many factors brought about a deterioration of this great resource, but it is being brought back by the conservation department's lake reclamation program in which the coarse fish are eliminated and original trout populations reintroduced. The program, over a period of years, can be easily helpful in increasing public use of the preserve, especially the more remote areas.

Part of this program, however, must consist in the purchase of more lakes and streams by the state, a matter in which we are very lax. Tied into this program must be better access to existing state lakes, and by this I do not mean more roads, but rights to go across private property to reach state lands.

I am not disparaging present fishing possibilities in the preserve.

There are hundreds of lakes and thousands of beaver ponds affording excellent opportunities to those who will walk. And it is still possible to catch two- to five-pound native brook trout in lakes completely surrounded by the state land, back in the deep woods.

In the past decade, mountain climbers and hikers have greatly increased the use of the preserve. These numbers are, however, just a trickle compared to the number of those who will, a decade hence, be enjoying the long trails and the magnificent High Peak country of the Adirondacks and Catskills.

A book has come off the press this week called *The Adirondack Forty-Sixers*. It outlines the progress of those who have stood on top of all of the forty-six peaks of the Adirondacks over four thousand feet in height. (Two in the Catskills also exceed this height.)

More than a hundred individuals have accomplished this feat, most of them in the last few years. Two of this group—a boy from Watertown and a girl from Schenectady—had completed the requirements by the time they were ten years old. Such accomplishment speaks well for the determination of the climbers. It also makes nonsensical the claim that the forest preserve is "locked up" or is nothing more than a "jungle for wild animals."

More than six hundred miles of trail are marked in the High Peaks region, and along this trail system are scores of open log lean-tos. We need more of this kind of development.

But we also need areas where no development of any kind, including trail marking, is permitted. There are ten thousand miles of good foot trails leading to all lakes, mountain valleys, and to all remote hunting and fishing areas. It is desirable that there shall always be places where a compass and a good guess is needed if we are to reach our destination.

It goes without saying that motorized vehicles and plane traffic should be eliminated from the major wilderness regions, and that a system of pack-horse traveling and conveyance of hunters into remote areas by horse-drawn vehicles is both desirable and permissible under the law.

It will be unnecessary for me to go into the subject of winter sports, such as skiing, snowshoeing, and all the attendant uses of the preserve. We have settled state policies with respect to such developments as Whiteface, Gore, and Bell Aire mountains. And the winter sports recreation other than these specialized centers will increase, as it rightly should, but only as fast as enterprising Adirondack and Catskill people provide good and hospitable convenience for the public.

In my opinion the number of resorts in the Adirondacks with the

"Swiss-like" atmosphere of warm hospitality is very small. This presents a very great challenge to the enterprising resident of the Adirondacks.

Dean Joseph Illick has recently stated very correctly that the misinformation about the forest preserve is widespread. I think such misinformation is appalling, especially when people not fully informed with respect to the character of the lands comprising the forest preserve recommend lumbering them!

For many years, the policy of the state was to buy lands nobody wanted, the burned and devastated lands, the cut-over and inaccessible lands. In 1910 when the forest preserve comprised 1,643,000 acres, Conservation Commissioner H. Leroy Austin said: "Except recently, and in the Catskill region alone, the state has made no effort to seek out desirable purchases and to consummate the same, but has depended entirely upon voluntary offers and as a result has in most cases purchased only such lands as could not be sold to anyone else."

Happily this policy has long since changed, but the basic land ownership of the forest preserve remains somewhat the same. And even today, the best lands for forest growth are still in private ownership and subject to forest management.

In my opinion, the estimated dollar value of the existing saleable timber on the forest preserve is worth only a fraction of the inestimable values of an inviolate forest for watershed protection and forest recreation.

In an excellent booklet just issued by the Department of the Interior and the National Park Service, *National Park Wilderness*, there is the following statement:

> The National Park Service immediately rejects such proposals, (stock grazing, lumbering, prospecting and mining, and hundreds more) and it requires no rare understanding of park objectives to make the decision. . . . The wilderness proper serves all park visitors. Those who penetrate it gain its fullest rewards. But, it is the part of a national park that is not intensively used that makes it a park, and the undeveloped wilderness beyond the roads furnishes the setting and the background. Take away the background, and the park atmosphere of the whole disappears, and with it a very large part of the pleasure of those whose only contact with wilderness is experienced as they look outward over it from the roadside. Wilderness areas, and the quality of wilderness which must pervade the most visited part of a national park, are a primary resource—a

resource to be cherished and guarded, a resource whose benefits each park visitor is entitled to enjoy.

In conclusion, may I say that as conservationists we accept and support the state policy of timber production forests outside the boundaries of the Adirondack and Catskill parks. We are presently working on a long-range program to build up the state forests to the point where they ought to be for the economy of the state.

I met Assemblyman Robert Watson Pomeroy *(right)* at the airport before we left to survey Adirondack lands. A flight around the "blue line" boundary of the Adirondacks revealed that substantial tracts of land, including mountains, lakes, and forest, were not within the park. Legislation soon added one hundred thousand acres of very important country to the Adirondack Park. Photograph courtesy of NYS Department of Environmental Conservation. Photograph by William Foss.

The Forest Preserve

A STUDY IN DEPTH

The most extensive and intensive study of the New York State Forest Preserve ever made in the Adirondacks and Catskills was carried on by the Joint Legislative Committee on Natural Resources for New York State during the period from 1951 to and including 1965. As an advisory member of that committee from its inception, I would like to put into the record of this constitutional convention a brief summary of the work of that committee, its scope, and its conclusions.

The New York State Forest Preserve has for many decades been the subject of great controversy. The principal reasons for this controversy are the following:

1. The Adirondacks and Catskills, with their abundance of lakes, forests, mountains, and streams, are unique in the world in the topography they possess.

2. The vastness of the area of the parks—more than nine thousand square miles—has limited a cohesive understanding of the physical nature of state lands and their relationship to private lands.

3. The proximity of some thirty-five million people to these lands has resulted in great pressures upon these regions, which enjoy an absolutely unique protection by the state constitution.

4. As a result of the great controversies over use of the forest preserve, the Joint Legislative Committee on Natural

Reprinted from a statement to the New York State Constitutional Convention, Albany, New York, May 24, 1967.

Resources was created in 1951. The late Assembly Speaker, Oswald D. Heck, acutely aware of the lack of basic data on the preserve, caused the creation of the committee, and he was instrumental in seeing that a very wide spectrum of interests were brought together for the study.

Senator Wheeler Milmoe chaired the study from 1951 until 1959, and Assemblyman (later Senator) Robert Watson Pomeroy continued the program after Mr. Milmoe's retirement. Both men provided outstanding leadership and their dedication in getting the facts before the people was above reproach. The committee was bipartisan in the best sense of the word and during the principal fourteen years of its life had an advisory group of about twenty citizens from the most diverse interests in the state. Some of these members were Dean Hardy Shirley, State University College of Forestry; Lithgow Osborne, former conservation commissioner; Karl T. Frederick, founder of the State Conservation Council; Dr. Gustav Swanson, Cornell University; Lyman Beeman, Finch Pruyn, and Company; A. Augustus Low, Empire State Products Association, and many more of similar stature. It was an advisory committee in fact and not just in name. The meetings revolved around this group, and as a result they were religiously attended by all members.

Scores of full-day meetings were held, principally in Albany. Overnight inspection trips of the Adirondacks and Catskills were frequent. Elk Lake, Saranac Lake, Speculator, Indian Lake, DeBruce, and Cold River were just a few of the places visited. Wilderness areas, demonstration forests, and game-management projects were included in the itinerary. They were guided for the most part by experienced administrators and technicians of the conservation department.

Many of the nation's foremost foresters and conservation experts testified before the committee: key men from Michigan, Wisconsin, Pennsylvania, and Washington came to record their judgments and experiences. Eminent wilderness advocates as well as the nation's best foresters and scientists were heard. There were always reports that followed for study or for full-scale debate by committee members. Let it not be thought that such meetings were always harmonious—at times they bordered on the violent! The most controversial issue was the question of lumbering the forest preserve. Studies substantiated the fact that for the most part the best tree-growing lands in the park remain in private ownership and are either being lumbered or are subject to be. They also emphasized the fact that a large percentage of the forest preserve is mountain slopes, where extremely thin soil characteristics pre-

Lithgow Osborne at Elk Lake during a cross-park junket in 1962. "The principal uses of the forest preserve, each of utmost importance, are to be regarded as watershed protection and public outdoor recreation of a type that is consistent with the preservation of natural conditions"—Conclusion of a fifteen-year study, 1965, Joint Legislative Committee on Natural Resources for New York State.

vail and where the highest possible use of the lands is for the protection of the sources of our principal rivers and streams.

Of inestimable importance were the continuing field studies headed by Dr. Neil Stout of the College of Forestry at Syracuse University and

Clarence Petty of the New York State Conservation Department. The projects and studies included wilderness journeys into the farthest and most remote regions, the climbing of mountains and the canoeing of rivers. There were summer-long adventures by professional research men who inventoried not only the physical characteristics of the vast regions involved but also the beauty of the lakes and streams and mountains they saw.

The work of this field crew, as well as that of the committee, was compiled each year in a book published by the state. Gradually there came into being a strikingly clear and accurate picture of the forest preserve. It verified the uniqueness of this vast public domain—one of the nation's largest—and it also pointed up the problems.

As the data gradually accumulated and the field men dissipated myths and fables about the region, an incredible thing happened: committee members began to realize that as widely different as their individual philosophies might be, two things were true:

> 1. No committee member could claim his devotion to the forest preserve was more sincerely in the public interest than any other member.
>
> 2. Areas of agreement on fundamental objectives became larger as arguments brought out the precise reasons for positions assumed.

The list of legislative actions by the committee and its educational accomplishments are too long for inclusion now, but a few of them are outlined here:

> 1. The mapping and description of the sixteen large wilderness regions of the Adirondacks and Catskills
>
> > This has permitted the state to focus attention on the more important areas and to consider special protection for them, including the banning of motor vehicles for such tracts.
>
> 2. The enacting of legislation that put a halt to a constant loss of forest preserve lands due to faulty title
>
> > More than 100,000 acres were lost to the preserve before this legislation was enacted.
>
> 3. The enlargement of both the Adirondack and Catskill parks to take in the most significant mountain and lake country of these two regions

This resulted from the committee's aerial survey of the park's "blue line."

4. The passing of legislation that effectively made possible the improvement of arterial roads in the parks and at the same time prevented further fragmentation of the wilderness

This included the amendment that kept the Northway from penetrating the Pharoah Lake Wilderness. Incidentally the route, which was approved finally, was declared in 1966 to be the most beautiful highway in America.

5. The supporting of public campsite and trail programs as administered by the New York State Conservation Department and the backing for necessary financial aid for this program

6. The support of the timber production forests of the state and of a better forestry service for private landowners

7. The in-depth study of the various court decisions and attorney generals' opinions from 1895 to the present

The committee's studies concluded that almost any reasonable proposal for use of the forest preserve by the people was permitted under the law and that vastly more latitude had been authorized than was generally known.

8. Above all the committee brought into focus the relationship of forests to water, the economic value of wildforest land to the state, and the historic significance of the Adirondacks and Catskills to the United States.

In 1963 the committee proposed a statement of public policy that was unanimously adopted. The policy stated:

1. That the principal uses of the forest preserve, each of utmost importance, be regarded as watershed protection and public outdoor recreation of a type that is consistent with the preservation of natural conditions.

2. That the preservation of its natural conditions under the constitutional protection of Article XIV be continued as fundamental policy.

3. That the further construction of foot trails, lean-tos, and public campsites be encouraged as need develops, but that such fa-

cilities as campsites and picnic areas be located outside of any defined wilderness areas such as those recommended in the 1961 report of the Joint Legislative Committee on Natural Resources.

4. That the conservation department take such action as may
be necessary to regulate or, if necessary, prohibit the use of motorized equipment wherever the wilderness character of the forest preserve is threatened thereby.

5. That continuing studies of wildlife habitat improvement be
conducted by the conservation department and that appropriate action, consistent with the constitution, be encouraged to preserve
and enhance our wildlife resources.

In my opinion, the work of the committee underscores the value
of Article XIV of the New York State Constitution which we hope this
convention will reaffirm unchanged. The documentary record of the
committee is available to all, and it forms a solid base on which this
convention can rest its case.

Statement to the Adirondack Park Agency

The proposed Adirondack Park State Land Master Plan as advanced by the Adirondack Park Agency is, for the most part, a well-designed guide for the protection and enhancement of the New York State Forest Preserve.

I am aware of the problems the agency faced in putting together a plan which would satisfy the diverse interests of the people of our state. To a very large degree you have accomplished this difficult task.

Many of us are particularly pleased to note the emphasis you have put on the fragility and irreplaceability of the forests, rivers, streams, and lakes which are so uniquely combined in the Adirondack Mountains.

While the proposed master plan is undoubtedly the best combination of detailed recommendations for the forest preserve made in the long history of the park, there are several refinements which conceivably would substantially improve it.

My first suggestion relates to the Moose River Plains with which I am very familiar. Those of us who fought and defeated the proposed Higley Mountain dam, which would have inundated most of this region, have been upset over the misuse of this region and the decimation of its once abundant wildlife because of certain management practices. Personally I would favor the entire Moose River Plains region being made part of the West Canada Lakes Wilderness. Lacking this desirable objective, the least that should happen in this area is that Beaver Lake, Squaw Lake, and Indian Lake be made an integral part of that wilderness. The northern boundary near the plains should be the South Branch of the Moose River east to Otter Brook, thence up Otter Brook. This is an absolutely essential requirement to make the West Canada re-

Reprinted from a statement made at the Lake George Public Hearing, 1972.

gion a truly great wilderness. No management problems should be so important that they would deprive this wilderness of these three splendid lakes and their surroundings. Only a relatively small acreage is required for this addition.

In like manner, the Five Ponds Wilderness should include at an early date the proposed primitive area west of the Oswegatchie River. The truck trail involved should be one of the first roads to be eliminated.

The history of roads, jeep trails, and fire-truck trails in the Adirondack reflects the fact that they are the greatest single threat to wilderness that exists. The language in the first three paragraphs under this heading in the report is, in my opinion, too permissive. Such roads or trails are the primary reason why the wilderness regions as proposed are not larger and much more meaningful.

No part of the master plan is more important than this phase of it. The major problem in maintaining the wild-forest character of the entire park is involved in the extraordinary system of rivers which radiate outward from the center of the park to all points of the compass. To successfully carry out the original recommendations of the Adirondack Study Commission as they relate to these rivers will be to accomplish the highest single objective the agency is capable of achieving.

By these remarks you understand my support for your master plan. I believe the several refinements suggested will vastly improve your proposal, and I sincerely hope you will consider them favorably.

Just a few final words.

Your proposed master plan is, in reality, the crystallization of Adirondack studies which began in a serious way in 1951. The Joint Legislative Committee on Natural Resources, the Joint Legislative Committee on River Regulation, and numerous conservation committees of the senate and assembly have all contributed basic data for this final effort of the agency. Your work is consistent with the best conclusions these study groups came up with, and I am sure that you have made good use of their data and recommendations. But I feel it is only fitting that we should recall the names of some of those whose efforts made this present situation possible. They include men like Speaker of the House Oswald D. Heck, Lieutenant Governor Frank C. Moore, Senator Robert Watson Pomeroy, Assemblymen Leo A. Lawrence, Glenn Harris, Larry Lane, and Senator Bernard C. Smith. Nor should we overlook the great contributions made by Senator Francis Mahoney and commissioners of conservation such as Lithgow Osborne and others. Perhaps this suggestion will recall to each of you many other men and women who, in a very real sense, are a part and parcel of this magnificent job you are doing and will inspire you to carry on the heritage of vision they all bequeathed us.

Lost Pond. To preserve this land for the youth of tomorrow is to bequeath a heritage of incalculable value.

This is Your Responsibility

The clerk of the New York State Senate has just announced the defeat—by three votes—of a most vital Adirondack conservation measure. We who had worked for many months, devoting what seemed to be endless hours in behalf of this reasonable and urgently needed legislation, were stunned by the result. We had hardly expected as much support as we received in the assembly, although we had been reasonably confident that the upper house would back this meritorious bill.

We walked through the historic corridors of the capitol with the sure knowledge that we could have succeeded, for the margin of failure was so narrow.

Then it occurred to us that perhaps we could learn a lesson from this defeat. Who was responsible for it?

We determined to find out at once. We checked the clerk of the senate for a list of those who voted against the measure. Picking the first senator on the list, we immediately went to his office and requested an interview. This was granted, and we briefly stated our mission.

The senator was brief and explicit. "My constituents have not indicated to me that they wanted this measure. I have received no data favorable to it. I have received data against the bill."

This was incredible, since one of our most active conservation units was in this senator's district. They had made their position known far beyond the borders of their county and had been of inestimable assistance in forming the statewide committee sponsoring the measure.

A few days later, we received confirmation from our friends in the senatorial district in question that through a most unfortunate oversight their position had not been made known to the senator; that all the

Reprinted from the *Forest Preserve*, February 1949.

data and a statement of their position still lay on the desk of their legislative committee chairman. Hundreds of informed conservationists had relied on club action and no one had functioned in their behalf!

Subsequent checking revealed that several similar instances had cost us the victory; our friends had fought admirably in the field, convincing their friends and numerous clubs of the rightness of the issue, but they had failed to carry through to the required conclusion. Apparently everyone was informed except their elected representative who, in the last analysis, was the only man who could actually do anything about righting the unwise law!

In the current issue of the *Forest Preserve* are listed your senator, assemblyman, and the legislation together with introductory numbers identifying it. Would it be difficult for you to call your legislator on the phone now, presenting him with your personal position on the issues involved? And could you not follow this up with a letter to him? Of course you could do both of these things easily.

This conservation battle is your battle!

Your land, the forest preserve, is being invaded. Your personal rights are being transgressed. The heritage you should bequeath to posterity is being endangered. The possibility of enhancing the Adirondack and Catskill parks is yours, if you will act.

How can you evade this personal responsibility? By your failure to act you can make the most intense efforts of your fellow conservationists become utterly meaningless. By adding your voice to the gradually increasing numbers who have now determined to make this issue a personal one, you are strengthening the perilously thin line that is forming the bulwark against the devastating apocalypse of lost rivers, of drowned forests, and of vast and desolate mud flats.

To do so will give a new meaning to the summer's day you walk down the winding trail leading to Nameless Pond. As of old, there will be the bewitching fragrance in the air of balsam and spruce and of freshly growing things. There will be the melody of the wild forest—the song of the thrush, the chatter of red squirrels, the tinkling of falling water, and perhaps a flash of dun as a deer bounds off through the woods. . . . You will remember the bitterness of winter when the drab uncertainty of devastation hung chill and cheerless over this bit of Adirondack lowland. All of this had been scheduled to become a cemetery of stumps, a limbo of desolate mud flats!

But now, as you walk down the shadowed trail where shafts of sunlight pierce the green canopy of the trees, spotlighting a forest floor rich with ferns and flowers and mosses of the deep woods, you will recall the smallness of your effort compared to the greatness of the accomplishment you have made possible. Somehow the forest preserve will seem to be more your very own, and kinship with all the great out-of-doors will seem more real.

7

One Wilderness

The lure of the old log cabin on the edge of the wilderness has been irresistible.

Looking at the Adirondacks from the vantage point of having backpacked them for sixty years, I must conclude that I have but a fleeting glimpse of its magnificent ten thousand square miles. It is a view that understands to a reasonable degree the place names and major natural features of the region, a view that has seen much wilderness but actually knows relatively little of it—the way a wilderness in fact can be known.

I've stood on many high peaks surrounded by scores of miles of wild splendor. The tremendous cliffs of Indian Pass have awed me, rising as they do a thousand feet above the rock-strewn base. I have been enthralled by the perfections of nature along the Indian River in the West Canada Wilderness. I was in the canyon of O.K. Slip Falls in freshet time one May morning when its mist was a rainbow, and its roar, echoing between the vertical cliffs, was emphasized by the collapse of a section of the canyon wall nearby. These experiences of wild places have been inspiring. But they do not surpass the richness of One Wilderness I know. For I do possess a universe of wilderness!

It is a land beyond my ancient log cabin in the east-central Adirondacks, a land within the lake and river boundaries of the 170-square-mile Siamese Ponds Wilderness. Only a few trails penetrate it —and they lead to splendid recesses of solitude. Beyond those recesses are forests seldom trod by man.

This is a land of mountains, cliffs, caves, cataracts, and ancient wetlands. A land of remnants of virgin hardwoods, giant spruce and balsam, yellow birch, beech, hemlock, and elm. And of ranks of canoe birches that bend gracefully with vagrant winds. Of lovely fern-bedecked high mountain ledges deeply rutted with deer trails. It is a land of lakes—sixty-seven—one quite forgotten, where the music of running streams fills a shadowed glade, and where three tiny lakes jewel the top of a forgotten mountain. It is a land where beaver have created oases of sunshine in an otherwise unbroken sea of trees. A land of the deer, the bear, the otter, the fisher, the marten, the bobcat, the coyote—of the loon, the grouse, the pileated woodpecker, and flights of chickadees. A land of ferns and mayflowers, of trillium, violets, trout lily, and Indian pipe. And once in a while, always unexpected, of cardinal flowers illuminating a languid stream. It is a land where nature has all but obliterated any evidence of the pioneers who sought to subdue it.

In my mind's eye, I am atop a ridge of Diamond Mountain, on a ledge of its cliffs about five miles westerly of my cabin's clearing. Upstream a mile or so is our hunting campsite, close beside a tumbling brook born on the heights a thousand feet above. From this cliff, I see southwesterly a grand profusion of mountains, hills, and valleys with no evidence of man's intrusions. I look downward about a thousand feet to Diamond Brook which is dappled with sunlight as it hurries through the forest to a wild river downstream.

Across the valley is miles-long Cataract Mountain. On official maps this is labeled Eleventh Mountain, but I have always referred to it as Cataract Mountain because of the number of beautiful cataracts that course downward. Its trailless summit is more than three thousand feet above the waters of Lake Champlain thirty-five miles northeasterly. It looms dark and forbidding, but it invites exploration. Its great jagged cliffs are nearly covered with evergreens clinging to the fissures in the rock and growing undisturbed by man since the ice age thousands of years ago. Its skyline of giant spruces is still ragged from the fury of the land hurricane of 1950. I can hear the low rumble of one of its many cataracts which pours crystal waters over a ledge and splashes on great boulders by a tiny meadow below.

Everywhere I look, and in the vast country nearby that I cannot see, are memories of adventures with deer and bear. Everywhere are memories of my companions of half a century, their personalities and reactions to the many frustrations and triumphs they have experienced in this wild country. Who could possibly forget those long evenings in the warm shelter of our tents exploring each others lives and hopes and dreams? Those priceless hours recall adventures in the Arctic tundra, in the High Sierra, the Canadian bush, and even of blood and mud in the trenches of Normandy. There is contentment here, whether a storm rages, or winds whip the canvas, or snow bends it down, or whether the whole country is drenched in moonlight. And when hunting success is evident on the game pole, there is the tantalizing fragrance of venison cooking. Although only thin canvas shields us from the elements, there is a wonderful sense of well-being in a world that is being so brutally pillaged and torn asunder. Here, completely engrossed in nature, we find tranquillity and peace of mind. We do not pine for other times or other places. A world of adventure surrounds us.

Now I am remembering that day when we were lost in dense fog.

A gaggle of geese seemed to be lost also as we heard them circling around and honking overhead. We put on a hunting drive in territory which seemed strange to us and placed our men by compass bearings only. Unbelievably we got a monarch of a buck just before the sun dissolved the fog to reveal our location.

And there was that brilliantly clear November day, during a major crisis in the Panther Mountain dam battle, when with my companions I searched in vain for our well-known Elm Hill and could not see it because we were standing on top of it.

Another day, while on watch on Hardwood Ridge, a black fox leapt upon a nearby boulder, looked at me defiantly, and disappeared in a flash. Then there was the time when a hawk exploded from forest treetops to catch a red squirrel about twenty feet distant, and with its eyes full upon me flew cleanly through a balsam thicket and was gone. Unforgettable was that day when a great buck, cornered on a high mountain ledge, rushed past me just a few feet away, antlers gleaming in the sunlight, muscles working like pistons, and leapt off a thirty-foot cliff to his freedom. Who could imagine my reaction to such experiences and share my sense of awe and admiration for the creatures' courage and sagaciousness.

One early morning in June, my friend Rey Wells and I reached a beaver pond just in time to see a brook trout arch the still waters even as a beaver splashed a warning to its young nearby. The fish were biting, but neither of us will ever forget the way we were driven out of that lovely place by unimaginable hordes of black flies, deer flies, and mosquitoes. Right after the Second World War, another close friend and I found a remote beaver pond fed by a cataract, where for three summers we filled our creels with trout and never saw another fisherman. Our only problem there was that the hollow log above the pond where we stashed our equipment was regularly raided and scattered through the woods by a bear.

How can I forget those glorious hours sixty years ago when an old guide paddled me in the dark of night around the shores of a star-drenched lake back in the deep woods just to see the "critters" as they came down to drink. Or the night we roasted some of his venison—and talked before the campfire in front of the lean-to as owls hooted and a snowshoe rabbit periodically came into the firelight from the shadows. Then, quite suddenly it seemed, we saw the first lights of dawn come stealing over the mountain.

One must see this country in freshet time to really understand it. Brooks are overflowing, rivers and cataracts are roaring with white water, and the lovely shad bush is in bloom. You must feel what it is like to stand on storm-swept mountain peaks when the splendors of October are spread in a riot of color to far horizons and no words to describe its beauty will come to you. Or look up from your sleeping bag on a bitterly cold winter's night into a heaven foaming with stars, and as the wind sifts snow upon you, and wonder what on earth ever possessed you to be there alone just because you heard the mountain calling you. Then you will marvel at the intricacies of nature as fashioned by the Divine Artist and try to comprehend His work down through the inscrutable ages.

The Siamese Ponds Wilderness Region

Few proposals made by any of the many fine conservation commissioners of New York State have such promise as the one made by Sharon J. Mauhs recently, which he has termed "Project Forest Preserve." He said, and I quote briefly from his statement:

> Recently I stated my determination to proceed with a study of the human use of the forest preserve, a study which I have termed "Project Forest Preserve."
>
> I have been moving ahead with this study. But before I go further, I want to make it abundantly clear that the basis of this study begins with a full realization of the fundamental law of the New York State Constitution, which says that the forest preserve be "forever kept as wild forest lands."
>
> The objectives we see are these:
>
> 1. To obtain more knowledge about our forests, our waters, and our wildlife resources in the forest preserve, and
>
> 2. To find the proper human uses of these lands and forests without impairing their wild forest character.
>
> The first areas of study I have designated are the Mount Marcy Wilderness and the Siamese Ponds Wilderness. I want to suggest measures that will accomplish the following objectives:
>
> 1. Safeguard forever the natural, wild forest character of the forest preserve, and build up, where feasible, the size of this great wilderness so that these wonderful lands can remain forever a challenge to generations to come.

Eight Years of Study and Action on the Development and Conservation of New York State's Natural Resources, Report of the New York State Joint Legislative Committee on Natural Resources, 1959; the genesis of this article appeared in the *Bulletin of the Adirondack Mountain Club*, July–August 1944.

Siamese Ponds Wilderness, one of sixteen wilderness tracts in the Adirondacks. Photograph courtesy of NYS Department of Environmental Conservation.

2. Determine where adequate additional public campsites are available on the perimeters of these regions and to determine where these additional campsites should be built.

3. Provide a means by which hunters, fishermen, campers, hikers, canoeists, and all who love the outdoors can more advantageously and properly use this great New York State Forest Preserve, the like of which exists nowhere else in the country.

Subsequently the commissioner asked several members of his advisory committee to proceed with studies of these two specific areas. It is about one of these regions, the Siamese Ponds Wilderness, that these remarks are addressed.

The Siamese Ponds region is in the east central portion of the Adirondacks. It is an area unbisected by roads, twenty-five miles long and fifteen miles wide, roughly a rectangle of which the villages of Wells, North Creek, Indian Lake, and Speculator are corners. The eastern half of the region is in Warren County, the western half in Hamilton County. It contains approximately fifty mountains running to about thirty-six hundred feet in elevation, fifty lakes, and hundreds of miles of streams. Some of the country is very spectacular. One mountain alone has six cataracts, some very unusual, fed by the springs in a large swamp near the summit.

The Siamese country is heavily forested. Three-quarters of it— 150,000 acres—is forest preserve, most of it acquired before 1900.

As might be expected, there are virtually all types of forests here. The high mountains are largely spruce-clad above elevation twenty-eight hundred feet. Below that elevation generally may be found the mixed hardwood-softwood forests which are typical of those which predominated in the Adirondacks a century ago. The valleys and often the relatively high plateaus have swamps, some quite extensive, of spruce and balsam. There are some regions with wonderful stands of hardwood—some of it virgin—birch, maple, and ash. Many ridges have extensive beechnut stands.

Throughout the region is a lushness of mosses and ferns. In mid-May one can walk all day through heavy hardwoods under which are countless acres of mayflowers. The trails are lined with white, yellow, and blue violets, red, white, and painted trillium, Dutchman's breeches, and Indian pipes.

Deer and bear are relatively abundant. Beaver are common. One four-square-mile area I know has twenty beaver ponds. In this type of country, such ponds are a boon to trout fishing, since the streams are fast-running and often run for miles without many sizable pools where trout can develop. Lately the wolf or coyote population has increased rapidly. It is no longer uncommon to hear these animals' plaintive bark in summer evenings. Fisher and otter are not too rare. All of the other wilderness denizens are here such as the bay lynx, snowshoe rabbit, red squirrel, and pileated woodpecker.

All of the many lakes have trails leading to them, some being old lumber roads and others just paths made by fishermen. Basically these are trout lakes. Some produce excellent fish. Others need the reclamation crew. A number of these are high mountain lakes which nestle more than two thousand feet above the sea. They present great opportunities for not only fine fishing but for never-to-be-forgotten wilderness adventures by fishermen or campers.

Three major state campsites are located near the outside perimeter of this region. One is at Sacandaga River near Wells, another at Speculator, and still another at Lewey Lake. It would appear that there ought to be a fourth near North Creek. There have been tentative plans for a campsite at Thirteenth Lake but more recently it has been advanced that this two-mile lake reaching down into the north central portion of this wilderness ought to be kept for informalized camping parties. The lake is almost four miles from the main North Creek-Indian Lake highway.

It is difficult at this point to estimate the number of miles of trails leading to the heart of this wild area from arterial roads. It is safe to say, however, that there are at least one hundred miles of such trails already in existence. It might be well to describe one of the many trails in existence.

Several miles south of Bakers Mills is an area known as Oregon which has substantial parking areas right at the beginning of the Siamese Ponds trail. This trail proceeds northerly over a spur of Eleventh Mountain and proceeds up the East Branch of the Sacandaga River to Thirteenth Lake about ten miles north. A branch of this truck trail goes to the Siamese Ponds some six miles in, and others lead to long-famous hunt camp meadows which were formerly logging camps. Curtis Clearing and Sawyer Clearing are two of these.

It is not uncommon to find thirty or forty cars of hunters with shoulder packs at Oregon on weekends during the big-game season when they head for their comfortable wilderness tents, two, four, or six miles back in. In most cases, teamsters have drawn in their basic equipment such as tents and food, and they are available for hauling out deer and bear.

It should be noted that the number of these organized wilderness hunting parties is constantly increasing as the knowledge of the singular advantages of such hunting become better known.

Larry Kohler, author of *Shots at Whitetails*, states that this is "real quality hunting." George Lessor, famous big-game hunter who holds a Boone and Crockett Club citation for the world's largest caribou, and who had hunted game all over the world says, "Adirondack deer hunting is the queen of big-game hunting." He says that the deer are truly wild and just sufficiently abundant to make success a real achievement. And of course, he counts the beauty of the country an important part of the adventure.

Any study of the human use of such a region as this should begin with gathering attitudes of people who live on the outside perimeter of the region. I am sure that such a study will be most revealing.

Basic to all studies, of course, are large-scale maps and aerial photographs. Trails need to be plotted, and the present use of the fishing and hunting resources known. Out of such a study will come crystal-clear reactions on which the most serious-minded people will agree.

This is the problem: to understand the physical aspects of the region and the present human use of it. Too long have we been generalizing about what ought and ought not to be done; it is time now to become specific and to come up with recommendations, which take into account the whole complex picture of mountains, forests, lakes, waters, wildlife, trails, ownership, accessibility, and existing human use.

Here is as great a challenge as conservationists have ever faced. For within this generation there shall be set a pattern which can either result in the substantial destruction of wilderness in the Adirondacks and Catskills or in securing a better-rounded, more adequate and more defensible wilderness for this generation and for posterity.

Hunting and fishing camp in the Siamese Ponds Wilderness, 1931. With civilization left far behind, all you have between you and the elements is a thin piece of canvas.

White Thunder

$\mathbf{W}$e stood on the bank of the East
Branch of the Sacandaga River, debating the merits of the situation. We
had come for trout, Irv and Nat and I, but a whole series of minor de-
lays had spent the afternoon until now scarcely more than an hour of
daylight remained for our hike to White Thunder, initial objective of
our overnight trip.

"It's just a case of common sense and good judgment," Irv suggested. "In fact, a child could make the right decision this time!" He
looked at the raging torrent of white water, a hundred feet across, but it
was easy to see that he was thinking of a little log cabin, dry and comfortable, just fifteen miles farther up the road on the same side of the
river.

The overcast sky threatened a rainy night. The air was damp and
cold. Nearly a week of almost constant rain squalls had soaked the land
until there was hardly a dry twig in a hundred square miles. Even as we
stood there the east wind shifted, and I sensed a change in the weather
as a fragrant breeze from the west swept across the river. It was time
for decision—a reasonable, judicious decision.

Hip-deep in the middle of the river, with a heavy pack making
good balance questionable, fish pole in one hand and in the other a
stout five-foot alder to help brace against the current, I began to wonder if ever, when challenged by the primal elements, I had actually
made a judicious decision! But it was much too late for reconsideration,
so we inched across the slippery rocks and finally reached the west
bank without serious mishap.

The trail looked inviting, and with every minute bringing night

Reprinted from the Newsletter of the Federated Garden Clubs of New York State, Inc.,
September–October 1946.

more completely upon us, we pushed up the trail which skirts the brook and listened eagerly for the falls.

We heard White Thunder for a considerable distance before we came upon this torrent of crystal water which drops off a cliff into a deep, dark pool, where, churning madly, it whips up foam clusters two feet high and dashes off at right angles down a rocky gorge to the river. Reaching the ledge above the falls, we threw off our packs and in the dim light beneath the great trees, cast a white bucktail into the foaming waters.

A speckled beauty grabbed it after a few casts and dove for the deep waters under the falls. There he snagged the line before recovery was possible, and a new leader and fly required more of those golden minutes before darkness. The next cast was more successful, and in a little while we had three trout ready for breakfast.

Nat had meanwhile prepared a side-hill camp beneath a great pine. Soon a campfire had transformed the gloomy woods into a cheerful home, and we were luxuriating in the simple joys of forest life. We lingered long over coffee with fixings and then slipped into our sleeping bags.

The woods fairly resounded with the thunder of the waterfalls. All else was still. The dying campfire cast flickering shadows on the trunks of the stately pines, which seemed to rise indefinitely towards the sky. Occasionally a star gleamed through the entwining lacework of branches, as the wind moved the lofty crowns and sent vaporous clouds hurrying eastward toward the ocean. How wonderfully remote seemed the land of rush and hurry we had so recently left! How inexpressibly grand to lose oneself so quickly in this land of trees and rocks and crystal waters, and to become again, for just a little while, brother to the deer.

Dew had heavily covered our sleeping bags by dawn. We were up at first light, and after a hearty breakfast we cached our packs and headed up the brook toward the beaver dam and glacial lakes.

Have you ever stood in the center of a beaver dam in the hush of an early June morning, breathlessly joining your rod and begrudging every second it was taking? There was the placid surface of the black water, reflecting the peculiar beauty of the drowned land and the white cliffs of the enclosing ridge to the west. There was the rhythmic drum of a woodpecker on an ancient dead spruce by the beaver house; a black duck wheeled in flight and dropped into the water beyond the reeds.

At last you were ready. Carefully, oh, ever so carefully, you cast into the water—there where it seemed the original stream channel surely must have been. The lure hit the water with an almost imperceptible splash which caused ringlets of water, in undulating waves, to spread out upon the surface of the pond. Breathlessly you waited. The lure settled gradually, inch by inch.

Suddenly with a strike you felt clear to your toes, a trout straightened the line, weaved this way and that, and headed for deep water. You let him take it an instant; then you set the hook. Swiftly you work him to you, reeling fast. Now he's almost at your feet, twisting and dodging, orange and white churning the water. Then the net, and you have him, the most beautiful of fish, with a galaxy of color and symmetry of form unsurpassed anywhere.

Mix up such experiences with the loss of big ones, the snagging of hooks and leaders, and occasional success, and you will have found the hours are fleeting indeed.

Beyond the beaver pond, we came upon two little glacial lakes, smiling in the sunshine amid the quiet, green hills. An occasional giant pine rose majestically from the water's edge. A steady breeze rippled the dark blue water, while here and there in the placid coves a trout rose for an early fly.

We stood on the trunk of a giant pine which years ago had fallen into the lake and whose substantial girth some sixty feet out gave good footing for a fisherman. As I cast freely towards the lake's center, it occurred to me that it would be fun to fish even were there no fish here! But the trout hit spasmodically, and it was not long until we had the limit and the delightful satisfaction which comes with so doubtful an achievement.

The trip back to White Thunder was full of interest and enjoyment. For one soon learns that while his objective may be a creel of trout, a shank of venison, or a roll of film exposed to trees, lake, or woodfolk, this is but incidental to the more important whole, which is appreciation of all the little things that make up the great out-of-doors.

Even now I can hear the roar of the rapids at White Thunder and see a campfire flickering fitfully in the twilight beneath the towering evergreens. And I know that soon again I will cast upon the still, dark waters of that beaver pond, and catch, as always, the richness of the Adirondacks, whether it be a trout or the glimpse of a deer bounding off through the woods or yet the memory of a moccasin flower, growing shyly alone there by the side of the trail.

Johnny Morehouse, 1928. How can you describe a man who is part of the mountains?

Adirondack Fauna

It was one of those fine, sunny May days about halfway between maple sugarin' and trout fishin' when the old guide and I hiked off to the Dual Swamp country on the plateau south of Bog Meadow. About noon we had reached the cliffs above the snow-patched swamp and in a little rock cranny sheltered from the wind, we built a tiny fire of spruce twigs and had some "vittles."

No place can be more wild than Dual Swamp. When you walk through it, you are ankle deep in rich green moss. The ghostly tamaracks and spruce and balsam crowd one another in jungle- fashion and are thoroughly intermixed with tag alder and swamp brush. Well-defined game trails thread through the most impenetrable parts, occasionally climbing a hardwood hummock and then twisting away through a slough hole where the pitcher plant grows in such profusion.

Just below us lay a tiny pond—not thirty feet across—yet amply large to reflect the full beauty of Adirondack sky and the spired crowns of ancient evergreens.

"If this were a day fifty or sixty years ago, Johnny," I queried of my bewhiskered friend who had spent nearly all his life in these wild places miles from a clearing, "in what way would this scene be different?"

He thought a moment. The smoke of the campfire spired straight into the branches of some spruce clinging precariously to the cliff brink above us. From across the swamp came the shrill notes of a blue jay, while a solemn stillness hung over the swamp below us.

"The trees are the same, and the cliff and the swamp. Only one thing lacks of it bein' just the same."

"And that?" I questioned.

Reprinted from the *Cloudsplitter*, March–April 1949, by permission of The Cloudsplitter, Albany Chapter, ADK.

"Critter movement! This time of day is sleep time for most critters and allays has been," he said, "but even so there would be the movement of some of them in this swamp and woods. Some would be disturbed by other critters, some would be feeding and all of them would be less afeard than they be now. But you'd see some of 'em movin' out there now," he said as he pointed out across the land I had come to love so well.

I have often thought of this sage perspective when some of our so-called game experts try to convince us that the primeval forests of the northeast were almost barren of wildlife. Some of these people have assured us that a scarcity of wildlife was the rule then and that wildlife depends on the lumbering of the forests. We were inclined to listen with awe to these proponents of lumbering until we realized that much of the Adirondacks had already been lumbered at least once. If their conclusions were correct, these mountains would now teem with wildlife.

Then we came upon this considered statement of one of America's greatest wildlife authorities, E. W. Nelson, former chief of the United States Biological Survey, who disposes of such nonsense with this indisputable testimony:

> At the time of its discovery and occupation by Europeans, North America and the bordering seas teemed with an almost incredible profusion of large mammalian life. The hordes of game animals that roamed the primeval forests and plains of this continent were the marvel of the early explorers and have been equaled in historic times only in Africa. With this profusion of large game, which afforded a superabundance of food, there was also a corresponding abundance of large carnivores: wolves, coyotes, black and grizzly bears, mountain lions and lynxes. Fur bearers, including beavers, muskrats, land otters, sea otters, fishers, martens, minks, foxes, and others were so plentiful in the New World that immediately after the colonization of the United States and Canada a large part of the world's supply of furs was obtained here.

A fundamental cause of the decline of wildlife in the Adirondacks may be traced to the clearing and settling of the great river and lake valleys, which from time immemorial had afforded winter shelter and food for moose, elk, caribou, deer, and other animals. Unquestionably the Hudson, the Sacandaga, the Black, the Ausable, the Bouquet, the Saranac, and other valleys were favored retreats for these animals. They

I stood with Johnny Morehouse looking at Second Pond in the Siamese Ponds Wilderness, 1928. Below us was an unbroken wilderness—mountains, forests, waters, and mystery—rolling on and on
into the far horizon.

served in exactly the same capacity as does the valley of the South Branch of the Moose or the East Branch of the Sacandaga today.

Market hunting and indiscriminate slaughter by man as well as the gradual whittling down of extensive wild areas were contributing factors, as were devastating fires that swept over the High Peaks region in 1903 and 1908 in particular. A fire slash may give some temporary new food to wildlife, but in the Adirondacks such fires lead to erosion and complete loss of soil on the steep slopes. What wildlife, for example, exists on Rocky Peak Ridge? Or Mount Dix? Or Niagara? Here and there may be found a deer and some small animals but in the main such land is useless for an abundant fauna.

Radical changes in environment also eliminate animals from certain regions. Consider the once-famous Tahawus valley, southern gateway to the High Peaks, now scene of open-pit mining at Sanford Lake. Less than ten years ago, it was commonplace to see from ten to thirty deer from one's car along a ten-mile stretch of road from the Tahawus post office to Adirondac village. With the advent of the mining crew and the transformation of Sanford Lake into a polluted mud hole, the deer have virtually disappeared from this once beautiful land. In 1944 the Mount Adams fire observer made the incredible statement to me that during the entire summer he had seen but one deer, and he made frequent trips along the road just mentioned.

We are apt to wish to recall those long-lost days when the moose, the elk, and other forms of wildlife still roamed this Adirondack region in numbers. But we are also apt to forget that unless this generation adequately protects and enlarges the existing wild-forest lands, other interesting animals including the otter and the marten will also become nothing but a memory beyond recall.

DEFENDING THE WILDERNESS

was composed in 10 on 12 Sabon on a Merganthaler Linotron 202
by Eastern Graphics;
printed by sheet-fed offset on 50-pound, acid-free Booktext Natural,
Smyth-sewn and bound over binder's boards in Holliston Roxite B,
and notch bound with paper covers,
with dust jackets and paper covers printed in 2 colors
by BookCrafters, Inc.;
designed by Mary Peterson Moore;
and published by

SYRACUSE UNIVERSITY PRESS

SYRACUSE, NEW YORK 13244-5160